PRAISE FOR
50 Ways to Use YouTube in the Classroom

"This book provides terrific ways to rethink the defaults for how teachers and learners consume and create YouTube content. Patrick has packed in many practical and innovative approaches that can help deliver impactful learning experiences. Recommended."

—**Dr. Reshan Richards**, chief learning officer, *Explain Everything*

"*50 Ways to Use YouTube in the Classroom* is a must-have guide for every teacher looking to inspire and connect learning to the digital world their students inhabit. Patrick has written the perfect blend of how-to, lesson design, management, and workflow, connecting readers with digital resources for support and continuous updates to an ever-changing platform. While he calls teachers to action, to meet students where they are, I believe his book is designed perfectly to meet teachers where they are."

—**Lisa Highfill**, teacher, author of *The HyperDoc Handbook*,
YouTube Star Teacher

"*50 Ways to use YouTube in the Classroom* is the survival guide for teachers who are interested in using YouTube in the classroom for improved teaching and learning. Instruction, collaboration, and student creation are all prominent themes of the book, with lesson ideas for each. Patrick takes teachers from the basics of how YouTube works to pro tips in an easy-to-follow progression."

—**Steve Katz**, Tech Czar at stevenkatz.com and
author of *Teach with Video*

"As educators, we used to be the fount of all knowledge. Now that mandate has been passed on to the Internet, and our role as educators is changing dramatically. The role of educators is now to drive learning deeper by asking clever, rich, open, high-order thinking and Socratic questions.

"For many educators their source of information is via Google; however, for most learners their source of information is YouTube. This is not surprising, as watching a video clip on YouTube is a far more efficient and effective way of learning than having to read a large document/book, especially if you're not a very good reader. Using YouTube is not just about consuming resources, it is also about producing resources. Increasingly, our learners are creating rich content that reflects their new learning through the creation of YouTube clips. How long will it take us as educators to allow learners to submit assignments via a link to a YouTube clip?

"Watching a three- to five-minute YouTube clip seems to me like a far more efficient way of finding out the depth of understanding that a learner has around the work that they have been learning. Marking the YouTube clip is also a far quicker process than having to read an essay! Creating a YouTube clip also allows learners' peers to make comments on the work they have created.

"This concise and easy-to-read resource provides educators with an introduction to the potential of the critical resource that is YouTube. It is our contention that the production of YouTube clips to express understanding of new work that has been learned will completely replace written reports and essays in the not-so-distant future. Video media represents our understanding—along with that of our learners—far more effectively and efficiently and carries huge amounts of nuance and subtlety that are lost in a written presentation. It is also very hard to plagiarise someone else's video!

"I recommend this resource very highly and encourage educators to make use of it. Patrick presents these ideas in a language that all educators find straightforward and easy to follow, and I encourage educators to make use of them!"

—**Mark Treadwell**, author of *The Future of Learning*

50 Ways to Use YouTube

in the

CLASSROOM

Patrick Green

50 Ways to Use YouTube in the Classroom
© 2018 by Patrick Green

This book is available at special discounts when purchased in quantity for use as premiums, promotions, fundraising, and educational use. For inquiries and details, contact the publisher at press@edtechteam.com.

YouTube and the YouTube logo are registered trademarks of YouTube Inc.

Published by EdTechTeam Press
Cover Design by Genesis Kohler
Interior Design by My Writers' Connection

TPB ISBN: 978-1-945167-39-3
ebook : 978-1-945167-40-9
Library of Congress Control Number: 2017961169
First Printing: January 2018

Irvine, California

Contents

Dedication ix

Introduction xi

    How to Read This Book .... **xii**

    Accessing Supplemental Resources .... **xiv**

Chapter One: Getting Started with YouTube 1

    Hook Your Students 2

    Bring a Concept to Life 2

    Show an Experiment 2

    Explain a Concept 2

    Start a Discussion 3

    Filter and Find the Good Stuff 3

    Subscribe to Keep the Good Stuff Coming 5

    Bookmark Videos to Find Them Later 7

    Use Watch Later for PD on the Go (Or in Bed) 7

    Navigate Using the Guide 8

Chapter Two: Curating Content with Playlists 11

    Create a Playlist 11

    Edit and Organize a Playlist 12

    Annotate a Playlist with Notes Specific to Your Class 13

    Personalize Learning through Playlists for Extension and Remediation 13

    Save Time with the "Please Don't Make Me Repeat Myself" Playlist 14

    Host an All-Nighter Exam Review Session 16

Chapter Three: Teaching with YouTube 17

    Make Full-Screen Mode Your Default 17

    Embed a Video Within a Google Slides Presentation 18

    Trim a Video within a Google Slides Presentation 19

    Focus Students by Removing (Potentially Inappropriate) Distractions 20

Flipped Teaching: Assign a Video for Homework 21

Embed Video in a Google Form 22

Create a Photo Slideshow for Parents 23

Allow Students to Access Information in Their Native Language
with Subtitles 24

Crowd Source Videos Using a Collaborative Playlist 25

Loop a Video When Hosting Parents in Your Classroom 26

Record and Edit on the Go with the YouTube App 27

Make Sub Plans as Easy as Taking a Selfie 29

Archive Your Work 30

Use Privacy Settings to Give Access Only to the Right People 31

Keep Students Safe with Restricted Mode 32

Provide Family-Friendly Videos for Younger Students 33

Chapter Four: Setting Up Your Channel 35

Organize Your Content with a YouTube Channel 35

Brand Your Channel Banner with Custom Art and Links 37

Enable Longer Videos 38

Make Your Channel URL Memorable for Students 39

Produce a Channel Trailer to Educate Students and Parents about
Why You're Using YouTube 40

Promote a Timely Video by Featuring It on Your Channel 41

Manage or Disable Viewer Comments 42

Chapter Five: Creating Content with Advanced Tools 43

Manage Content and Access Creative Tools in the Creator
Studio 43

Save Time by Customizing Your Default Upload Settings 45

Bring in an Expert with YouTube Live Streaming 45

Broadcast a Classroom Event 47

Search for Copyright-Free Audio to Use Outside of YouTube 47

Check the Usage Rights of Popular Songs 49

Teach Content with a Screencast 50

Demonstrate a Piece of Software with a Screencast 52

Screencast a How-to-Use-an-App Video on a Tablet 53

Provide Feedback on a Student Assignment with a Screencast 54

Link to Other Important Info with Cards and End Screens 55

Attract More Student Clicks with Custom Thumbnails 56

Chapter Six: Empower Students to Create 59

Students Reflect on Their Learning Via Video 59

Students Self-Assess a Live Performance 60

Recapture and Repurpose Class Time with Recorded
Presentations 61

Students Create an Authentic Portfolio 63

Students Record Themselves Reading 64

Students Record Rough Drafts of Their Presentations 64

Provide Students with Actionable Feedback Via YouTube
Comments 65

Students Submit Video Evidence Meeting Criteria of a
Performance Task 65

Students Make a Movie 68

Students Make Thinking Visible with a Screencast 68

Assign YouTube Genre Mash-ups as Creative Tasks 69

Teach Students to Be Digitally Resilient through Managing
Comments 70

Teach Students about Copyright and Fair Use 73

Final Tip: Inspire Others by Sharing Your Creative Uses of
YouTube 73

Acknowledgments 75

More Books from EdTechTeam Press 76

Want more YouTube in the Classroom Tips? 83

About the Author 85

Dedication

For Oscar, who in kindergarten deviated from the norm: Instead of saying "doctor" or "lawyer," he set himself apart by declaring he wanted to be a YouTuber when he grew up. The other parents laughed, and your mom and I cheered.

Introduction

Teachers must meet students where they are. It's not just a mantra; it's a truth. And for this generation, which is used to unscheduled, ever-evolving online content packaged in short bursts and hyperlinked to even more content, it means taking a fresh look at how we use technology in the classroom.

Teachers can't know everything. They can't be experts on every aspect of their subject areas, and that's OK. In fact, many of your students will be a step ahead of you when it comes to new technology and global trends. But that's not an excuse—it's a challenge.

As a classroom teacher, you need to be nimble. You need to be responsive, and you need to harness the tools to which your students respond. You can't know everything, but you can continually update the formats and platforms you use to reflect the pulse of your students' culture, generation, and interests. For those of you who like to pull out the same file folder year after year, this challenge might sound daunting. Take heart: It isn't. There are secret agents you can employ to update your content and teach creativity, improve communication skills, capture student interest, and increase personalization. You don't have to get a doctorate— just open your browser.

Enter YouTube.

We live in a visual world. We live in a media-rich world. We know that great teachers use students' interests to maximize learning. We know that great teachers create authentic learning opportunities and use relevant tools. Great teachers meet students where they are, and YouTube is a tool to connect all those dots. YouTube is a classroom power.

If it sounds magical, that's because it is. Think about it: We learn by watching and doing. For centuries, people have relied on internships and apprenticeships to gain experience. YouTube is a treasure trove of tutorials. It's high-interest content, expert analysis, how-to videos, and so much more. It has a sky-high cool factor, and creators and thought leaders hang out there. That's the key—creators are always creating new content for you and your students to use, admire, and consider. It's a not-created-for-education tool that people utilize when they need to learn something new. It is used by creatives and professionals in all fields and is freely accessible to your classroom.

Today's teachers can find enormous opportunities on YouTube far beyond passive viewing and listening. It offers personalized, dynamic, and student-centered learning. It's important to remember that our students are different from previous generations, and with YouTube, we can bridge the gap between our knowledge and their needs, their popular culture, and their learning styles. We can model a growth mindset and take a continually evolving approach to learning as our tools change rapidly from day to day.

▶ How to Read This Book

YouTube is a creative marvel. To reach the place of using it with ease, we need to discuss a few nuts and bolts. If you're someone who runs from the words *web browser*, please hang in there. You can do this.

Unless specifically noted, this book refers to the desktop version of YouTube, the version you access from your desktop or laptop in a web browser such as Safari, Chrome, or Firefox. The mobile apps associated with YouTube on tablets and smartphones continue to expand and become more fully functional. If you can use YouTube on your desktop in a web browser, you can likely use it the same way in the YouTube app or the YouTube Studio app on your mobile device. But to keep things simple, this book will take a more general approach, sticking to the web browser interface.

I wrote this book for teachers of all age groups without regard to quality or quantity of access students have to digital devices. Some tips and strategies might need to be modified for your own situation, depending on the age of your students or how often you have access to creative tools such as tablets. In general, if you've got Internet access, if YouTube isn't blocked at your school, and you have at least one Internet connected device in the classroom, you're all set.

50 Ways to Use YouTube in the Classroom has six main sections: Getting Started with YouTube, Curating Content with Playlists, Teaching with YouTube, Setting Up Your Channel, Creating Content with Advanced Tools, and Empowering Students to Create.

I took care to organize this book in a manner that allows teachers to move through it in a linear fashion. You'll notice the skills build from basic use and functionality to more advanced content creation. At the same time, the organization of the book lends itself to jumping around. Feel free to use the Table of Contents to find the information you need when you need it. I encourage you to cherry pick the ideas, tips, and strategies as you need them. Here's a quick synopsis of each chapter:

Chapter 1: Getting Started with YouTube

With any new website or digital platform, it's smart to master basic navigation first. An orientation to the site and some basic search strategies will allow you to find the content you need. By the end of this chapter, teachers will have a greater understanding of how to customize YouTube to tailor to the personal interests and needs of their classrooms.

Chapter 2: Curating Content with Playlists

Learning to assemble playlists is a key piece of helping your students access the digital world. By creating, organizing, and annotating playlists, teachers can better personalize their students' learning and offer a variety of opportunities to all students.

Chapter 3: Teaching with YouTube

The tips in this chapter are practical and are aimed at helping you integrate YouTube into your classroom's regular routine. Many of these strategies will also move you closer to creating your own content.

Chapter 4: Setting Up Your Channel

Now that you have selected specific content for your classroom—or even created your own—you need to organize by learning some key features. From the basics of changing default settings to creative branding, we will explore ways to maximize your reach and better communicate with students and parents.

Chapter 5: Creating Content with Advanced Tools

At this point we will move beyond simple video recording and introduce tools that allow a teacher's creativity to really shine. You will learn about screencasting as well as live broadcasting, and you'll learn about more advanced functions hidden deeper within the YouTube Creator Studio.

Chapter 6: Empowering Your Students

Prior to this chapter, most everything is focused on how teachers might use YouTube. Here we will flip the focus onto students, examining ways to engage them in creating their own content, publishing, demonstrating knowledge, and reflecting on their learning. We will also discuss how to teach them to practice good Digital Citizenship skills.

▶ Accessing Supplemental Resources

I have also provided a few companion resources teachers might find useful. Because YouTube is always trying to improve, it could update certain features and change the layout of its site at any time. There is a good possibility that instructions contained in the book will soon be out of date. To make the book more timeless, I've avoided writing up too many detailed instructions and instead provided a website with some how-to videos. You can access this information in the following ways:

YouTubeClassroom.com

Typing this URL into your web browser will take you to this book's website, where you'll find links to the tutorials organized by chapter.

Pgreensoup YouTube Channel

YouTube.com/pgreensoup will take you to my YouTube channel where the tutorial videos are hosted and where I've organized them into playlists. I encourage you to subscribe to my channel so you'll be notified when future content is released—make sure you are signed in, and just look for a red subscribe button and click on it.

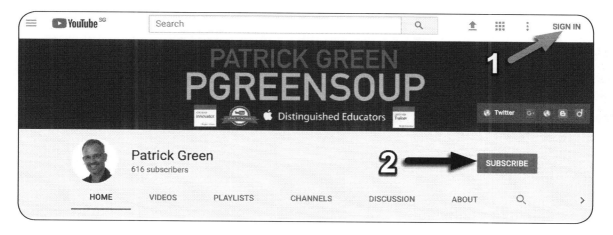

"Let Me Show You" QR Codes

There are QR codes scattered throughout the book which denote supplemental online tutorial videos. These codes come in handy for accessing the videos on your phone or tablet. Scan the code with your mobile device, and it will open the associated link, which, once you get used to it, is much faster and easier than typing out the entire URL. You'll need to have a QR code reader

app on your mobile device to scan the codes, unless you are using an iPad or iPhone with iOS 11, in which case you can simply use the default camera app. Give it a try on the code on the previous page to be taken to my YouTube channel.

Request More Tutorial Videos

While I've created a number of tutorial videos to accompany this book, I had to pick and choose. If there is a topic, tip or process you'd like to see in action, head on over to my YouTube channel and leave a request. I'll be continuing to publish tutorials and would love to know what people need.

▶ Leave a request at **youtube.com/pgreensoup/discussion**

Getting Started with YouTube

The most basic function of YouTube is to serve up videos for us to consume. As consumers of content, we use YouTube to pass the time, learn something new, or simply share a video with our friends. Before we can move beyond consumption and start using YouTube for creation, it is important to have a grounding in general video use in classrooms and how YouTube works in terms of basic navigation and organization. Let's get started.

The YouTube generation we find in our classrooms today is far more receptive to short, snappy videos than long teacher lectures. But as with any teaching strategy, you don't want to overuse video and thereby decrease its effectiveness. Take a quick spin through YouTube, and you'll see a variety of videos demonstrating just how versatile the medium can be. Skillful teachers can harness YouTube videos to engage students in a variety of ways so showing a video during class remains a fresh and welcome component. Here are a few of my favorite strategies for engaging students with video:

▶ Hook Your Students

Teachers who master lesson hooks know how to get their students to lean in from the start. Many teachers were taught to explicitly describe the hook as a component of lesson planning. Video is an especially effective way to draw students into a lesson by getting them to wonder about or question a particular topic. Some teachers show only a portion of a video at the start of class, asking students to predict what will happen next.

▶ Bring a Concept to Life

For many of our learners, seeing a concept in action or seeing an example of a concept conveys a deeper understanding than if the concept was simply explained to them verbally or read from a textbook. Throughout history, master teachers have modeled and demonstrated concepts in their classrooms, but when lack of funds or resources gets in the way, video can make the inaccessible accessible.

▶ Show an Experiment

Budgets aren't the only thing that get in the way of giving our students rich experiences. Sometimes the nature of what we are teaching is too dangerous to allow students to have a first-hand experience. Chemistry teachers surely can relate to this. YouTube videos can allow students an up-close look at things we want them to understand but not get too close to.

▶ Explain a Concept

Lecturing has earned its bad name through overuse and poor execution, but sometimes direct instruction is the best strategy. One way to keep things fresh is to let others do the lecture for you through video. Most teachers like to think they know their content well, but we can't all be the most knowledgeable person in the world on all the topics we teach. There is no shame in outsourcing your lectures to a video on YouTube, particularly one produced by folks with a whole creative team at their disposal. Just based on novelty alone, there's a good chance students will be more engaged in the video than a teacher lecture.

▶ Start a Discussion

Most teachers have structured a discussion around a text as a way for students to dig deeper into a topic while practicing collaborative and communicative skills. There is no shortage of protocols that can be used to get small groups discussing a topic. One benefit to using video over text is that you can ensure all students that are about to engage in the discussion have had access to the material without being hindered by their reading level. A short video followed by instructions on a discussion protocol is a great way to get students agreeing, disagreeing, and making connections.

Video is so versatile that it lends itself to many teaching strategies beyond those listed here. As you use video with your students and experiment with different strategies, it is important to remember that there can be too much of a good thing. Student engagement will stay high as teachers vary their approach to using video, keeping it fresh and in short doses.

▶ Filter and Find the Good Stuff

Using video in education is nothing new. Teachers have used video since its existence for a variety of purposes, but initially it required purchasing video from catalogs or setting a VCR (Yeah, remember those?) to record a television show. Using video in today's classroom has become a lot easier, with YouTube making seemingly limitless hours of video accessible. In fact, with so many videos out there, being able to find good educational content is an important skill. Thankfully, YouTube's powerful filters and search features allow teachers to find just the right video to meet their needs.

To search YouTube, you first need a basic understanding of how it works. Content creators—Disney, Jimmy Fallon, or your next-door neighbor—upload their videos to a YouTube Channel. All their videos reside on that channel and include additional data such as descriptions and keywords. Individual videos can also be organized into playlists, which are collections of videos grouped together by a user. One thing to note about playlists is that anyone with a YouTube account can create them; for example, on the Lego YouTube channel, Lego might organize some of its videos into a playlist called "Lego Friends 2017 Webisodes" to make it easier for fans to find those episodes all in one place. But any other user could create a playlist that includes some of these videos and title it whatever they choose, like "Videos To Use with Grade 5."

This basic understanding of how YouTube is organized will make finding videos much easier. Now you can use YouTube's advanced search filters to discover the right videos for your classroom by narrowing the search results. When you initially perform a search for a topic in YouTube, you get results that include individual videos, channels, and playlists all lumped together. By applying a filter to a search, you can be more precise and take advantage of some organization work that has already been done by others. Here is an example:

Let's say you teach chemistry. You search for the term *chemistry* on You-Tube and you get tons of stuff. But before you start clicking on videos, use the filter feature and filter the results to playlists. This will remove the individual videos from your results so that you're looking only at playlists—videos grouped together by other users according to a topic. Filtering can help teachers in multiple ways. You might find a playlist that was put together by another teacher, which might help you to zero in on the perfect videos for your class. Another way it helps is that you can see how other users have categorized videos, and you might change your search term accordingly. At the very least, you can utilize the work of others to weed out some of the junk and target potentially higher-quality videos that meet your needs. And if you are lucky, you'll see a playlist from a reputable channel that you recognize. In the chemistry example, two of the first ten playlists were created by CrashCourse and Bozeman Science, with which chemistry teachers might already be familiar and trust as producers of quality educational content.

Speaking of channels, try changing your filter from playlists to channels. By filtering to channels, you remove the individual videos and playlists, and you are now looking only at results of content creators who are publishing videos about chemistry. That means you can better locate channels to which you might want to pay attention in the future, channels that likely will continue to upload content in which you'll be interested. In the "chemistry" example, I'm again presented with CrashCourse, but I also recognize some other organizations that are reputable and worth checking out.

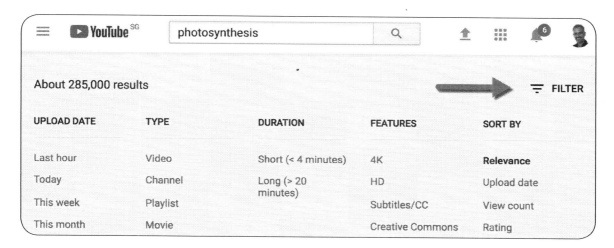

Filtering by playlist or channel is extremely useful to teachers in crowd-sourcing collections of videos and discovering content producers who are creating captivating videos appropriate for your students. But don't stop there! YouTube has a number of other search filtering options that are worth exploring, such as duration, relevance, and rating that can also help you find what you're looking for.

▶ Subscribe to Keep the Good Stuff Coming

The more you search YouTube for videos relating to the content you teach, the more likely you will begin to come across channels that are producing multiple videos that meet your needs. As you begin to recognize channels that are producing videos in your content area, you should subscribe to those channels. By subscribing, you are essentially telling YouTube, "I want more of this," and YouTube will oblige by sending you an update every time that channel uploads new content.

As you continue to subscribe to channels, you are letting YouTube know what you like. YouTube will continue to give you updates when your channel subscriptions upload new content, but it will also start suggesting other channels that you might like too. Each time you use YouTube, you are giving it information that it can use to tailor your experience. YouTube uses your channel subscriptions as well as your likes and watch history to suggest videos and channels it thinks you'll enjoy.

When you first open YouTube and are signed in, you will land on the home page, where you'll see new videos and channels related to your interests and use. YouTube assumes, if you are like most other humans, you'll click on something that piques your interest, watch it, maybe even like it, and perhaps go so far as to subscribe to the channel. As you interact with YouTube, it gets better and better at helping you discover content you can use to engage students and teach concepts.

Let's Practice Subscribing

Head on over to YouTube.com/pgreensoup and look for the Subscribe button. By clicking Subscribe, you are telling YouTube to inform you about any new content and to place it in front of you on your YouTube Home page.

SUBSCRIBE

▶ Bookmark Videos to Find Them Later

There is nothing more frustrating than knowing that at some point in the past, you've seen the perfect video for a specific lesson . . . but are unable to recall where you found it when that teachable moment arises. Fortunately, YouTube has a built-in Watch Later bookmarking feature to alleviate this pain. Users can click the clock that displays while watching a video or when viewing a video thumbnail, and the video will be saved in a default Watch Later playlist. This is the fastest and simplest way to keep track of the videos to which you'll want to return later for use with your students.

The Watch Later playlist is a bit of a multipurpose tool. You can use it as mentioned above, or, as its name suggests, to save promising videos for a more convenient time. As you use YouTube more frequently, you'll begin organizing videos with your own uniquely named playlists, but in a pinch the Watch Later playlist comes in handy.

▶ Use Watch Later for PD on the Go (Or in Bed)

Teachers are busy people, and every year there seem to be new priorities and new things to learn. Whether it's the Common Core—or its eventual replacement—or Professional Learning Communities or a curriculum refresh, faculty meetings and PD days seem to be filled with the priorities of other people. Schools talk a lot about personalizing learning for students, but what about teachers? You guessed it: YouTube has an answer. The Watch

Later button can instantly transform your smartphone from a Facebook-flipping device to a personalized professional-development delivery system.

The Watch Later function was designed as a way for users to quickly and easily keep track of videos they don't have time to watch but want to come back to later. By designating a video as Watch Later, users are adding videos to the one default playlist that is created for each user. There are multiple ways to add a video to Watch Later. From the YouTube home page, simply hover over any thumbnail and click on the clock icon that appears. From a video watch page, click the Add To icon as you would to add the video to any other playlist. You'll notice that Watch Later is always at the top of your playlist options. In the YouTube app on your phone or tablet, tap the More Options icon (the three dots that look like a caterpillar) and choose Add to Watch Later.

This Watch Later playlist is accessible on desktops from the YouTube home page, but the real power comes from accessing it on your mobile phone or tablet, where it resides within the Library button. If you commute on public transport, you'll always have a curated playlist of stuff you wanted to watch later queued up for some PD on the go. And while you'll have to alter your behavior a bit, instead of reaching for your smart phone for some pre-bedtime social media scrolling, hit the YouTube app instead to access your Watch Later playlist and some personalized PD.

▶ Navigate Using the Guide

Once you've started using YouTube while signed in, it will begin to customize your experience based on your interests and viewing history. The Guide is where you can find some of those customizations such as subscriptions and playlists. To access the guide, look for the three lines that resemble a rudimentary hamburger or a stack of three hotdogs. By clicking the Guide, you can toggle it open or closed. When open, you have access to links to your watch history, your Watch Later playlist, and your subscriptions. There are two sections below the main links, the Library and Subscriptions. In the

Library section, you'll see any playlists you've created or playlists you've saved that were created by others. In the Subscriptions section, you'll see channels to which you've subscribed with a number next to them noting the number of new uploads.

By understanding the basics of how search works within YouTube, you are now navigating the platform like a pro. And with subscriptions, you've customized YouTube to present you with more targeted and relevant content. Now that you've got so much quality content in front of you, it's time to start thinking about how to organize it.

CHAPTER TWO

Curating Content with Playlists

Now that you have learned how to search for playlists as a way to find great videos for your students, it's time to start curating this content—and organizing it to suit your specific needs—by creating your own playlists. Let's start with the basics:

▶ Create a Playlist

Remember, playlists are collections of videos organized by a user, which means you can do it however you want. You can create playlists using your own videos, videos from your favorite channels, or a combination of the two. As a teacher, you might consider organizing videos by topic, unit, standards, style, or even a compelling hook or discussion starter. Don't worry about planning your strategy ahead of time. You can always edit the playlist name later or add a video to multiple playlists when you think of a better way to organize. The main goal is to make playlist creation part of your workflow when browsing YouTube so you are developing a set of resources over time. After you get the hang of it, you'll be surprised at how quickly the content comes together. Starting a playlist is easy—just click the Add-To button under a video as you watch it.

One helpful way to get started is to create an "I Learned on YouTube" playlist. The more you use YouTube, the more likely it is that you'll turn to it when you need an answer to a "How do you . . . ?" question. By adding to this playlist, you'll have a record of all the things you learned on YouTube, and you'll avoid the frustration of being unable to find a particular video when you need it.

Duplex Printing on HP Laser Jet P1102

11,727 views   👍 54   👎 3   ➤ SHARE   ≡+   • • •

▶ Edit and Organize a Playlist

Teachers can use the editing features in a playlist to best organize the content for their students. All the options for tweaking the playlist are available once you open up one of your playlists from the Guide and then click the Edit button. Privacy settings and a few others are accessed by clicking the Playlist Settings button, but other features are hidden in plain sight and become available as you hover your cursor over the area to reveal more options; for example, you can drag videos into a desired order by hovering until the cursor turns to a cross, then just clicking and dragging.

You'll want to name the playlist appropriately, but you can always go back and change it later if you end up adopting new naming protocols. The description field can be used for additional details. If the playlist is for teacher use, you might leave yourself some notes on why you clumped these videos together, or the unit in which you plan to use them. If you plan to publish the playlist for student use, you could use the description field to give students an overview of what they'll find in the playlist or even to give them instructions for how to best use the playlist to support their learning. As with any video you create, you can adjust the privacy settings of a playlist for your intended purposes by choosing Public, Unlisted, or Private.

▶ Annotate a Playlist with Notes Specific to Your Class

I have found that the Notes feature is especially helpful to teachers. By adding notes to each video in a playlist, a teacher can create an educational context for videos that were not created with student instruction in mind. Here are a couple of examples of how a teacher might utilize this feature:

- ▸ Give instructions to students, alerting them to specific ideas to look for in the video.

- ▸ Ask students to make a hypothesis or prediction before viewing the video.

- ▸ Include a writing prompt for use after viewing the video.

- ▸ Add information or vocabulary that students might need to understand for the video to make sense.

- ▸ Include other context that might make a case for the video's relevance or inclusion as course material.

▶ Personalize Learning through Playlists for Extension and Remediation

No two students learn at exactly the same rate. Teaching would be a lot easier if they did. But chances are, if you are teaching on the planet Earth, you are facing a situation where some students are ready to move on and apply their learning while others are still struggling to acquire the basic vocabulary that will allow them to understand a new concept.

By creating playlists to provide extension activities for your advanced students, you can engage them in independent work while you focus on your students who need review or more practice. You'll want students to think deeply about the content they are viewing and apply it back to your class. Teachers can use the Notes feature to add a few questions to each video; for example, you might leave a note that says, "Using vocabulary from Chapter 4, describe what is happening in the first two minutes of this video." Or you could ask a more open-ended question to inspire your advanced learners to dig a little deeper or apply what they know in new contexts. You might even ask students to find other examples of a particular concept on YouTube and submit it to you. This option would allow you to update and refine your playlist for future students.

Playlists for remediation are similar, but in some ways easier to curate because you are looking to use more basic videos that repeat or simplify concepts for students. In many cases you'll be able to find videos created by someone else, and in instances where the perfect video doesn't exist, you'll need to create it yourself. (We'll get to that later when we discuss screencasting.) Having a playlist of basic concepts connected to any unit you are teaching allows you to give specific feedback to students as part of any formative assessment, directing them to the exact re-teaching they need.

Students will appreciate remediation playlists because they can review at their own pace, pausing and replaying each video until they can fully process the content.

By using playlists to differentiate for extension or remediation, you'll be able to spend more time with each group of students and be able to direct each student to the appropriate resource for the specific moment. The bonus is that your students will have their individual needs met rather than potentially missing out due to the one-size-fits-all approach.

▶ Save Time with the "Please Don't Make Me Repeat Myself" Playlist

If you aren't sold on using YouTube in your classroom just yet, hold on tight because you are about to become a believer. One of the best uses of playlists is creating a video collection that includes all the odds and ends of your course that are necessary or even, dare I say, uninteresting. You can view this playlist as the one that keeps you from having to repeat yourself over and over again. Maybe this list includes classroom procedures or expectations for recurring assignments. Good examples of what might be included in this playlist are safety rules for a science lab. Rather than lecturing little Johnny on what might happen to his eyeballs when he refuses to use the mandatory safety goggles, you can calmly say, "Johnny, please back away from the lab table, return to your seat, and review video number 1 in the 'Please Don't Make Me Repeat Myself' playlist." Of course, it will require time to create the videos you'll need for this playlist, but I promise you the effort will be paid back tenfold with the satisfaction you'll receive every time you have a chance to direct your students to this collection. And although not nearly as satisfying, this playlist will also come in handy for mid-year additions to your roster and any students who were absent for the initial information.

Patrick Green's
Please Don't Make Me Repeat Myself Playlist:

1. The Subtle Differences between Peer Feedback and Insults

2. Self-Assess: Is Your Interjection a Question or a Long, Boring Personal Story?

3. Safety Protocols: from Running with Scissors to Science Labs

4. Oh, You Forgot Your Pencil? I Wonder How You Could Solve That

5. Greetings for Your Teacher Other than, "What Are We Doing Today?"

6. Can You Go Early to Recess? No. But You Can Watch This Video When I Dismiss the Others

7. Formative Assessment Doesn't Mean Optional Assessment

8. Dancing, Talking Loudly, Making Farting Noises, and Other Ways Not to Enter the Classroom When You are Tardy

▶ Host an All-Nighter Exam Review Session

Some teachers host special exam review sessions outside of the normally scheduled class meeting time. It is always interesting to see who shows up. You'll get a mix of students, but you'll surely get a few who suddenly feel the urgency of learning the material into which they really didn't put much effort during the previous weeks. I'm always surprised by the sincerity of these students and how strongly they cling to the notion that they'll be able to learn everything we've covered in the last month in this final twenty-four-hour push. Brain research be damned; rather than getting a good night's sleep, these students try to cram for the test into the wee hours of the morning. With all-nighters inevitable, you might as well make a playlist that includes all the content that will be covered on the test. That way, at least you can sleep soundly knowing they are reviewing the right material.

Teaching with YouTube

Teachers around the world are integrating YouTube into their daily practice as they facilitate learning in their classrooms. In this chapter, we'll look at some tips and strategies that will help you harness YouTube for sharing and presenting information while also addressing privacy and safety concerns.

Additionally, we'll look at some YouTube functions that allow you to create a wide range of content from sub plans to photo slideshows. Let's start with a basic but extremely helpful tip:

▶ Make Full-Screen Mode Your Default

This is a #protip if there ever was one. Use Full-Screen mode whenever you're showing a video to the entire class. There is nothing that can ruin a teacher's reputation (and get students' eyes rolling) faster than fumbling around with basic YouTube controls like they've never been on the site before. Not only does Full Screen hide comments, suggested videos and other distractions, using it will earn you some street cred with the YouTube generation. You watch YouTube videos in your spare time—of course you do—and you're hip, so make sure your students know it by mastering Full-Screen mode.

To switch to a full screen, click the Full-Screen icon in the bottom corner of the video player. To exit out of full screen, press Esc on your keyboard or click the Full-Screen icon again.

▶ Embed a Video Within a Google Slides Presentation

While there are a number of presentation or slide deck tools out there, Google Slides works especially well with online videos and will come in handy when you want to present other information alongside a video; for example, you might want to have a couple questions for students to think about as they watch a video. Or perhaps you will show a short clip within the context of a larger presentation of information. Embedding a video within a Slide deck allows you to seamlessly transition from slides to video and back, and it has the added benefit of allowing you to share your presentation with the video included.

Inserting a YouTube video into a Google Slides file is easy. On any slide, just go to the insert menu and select video. You'll then be presented with the options to paste in the URL of your video or search for the video from within Google Slides. After the video is inserted, you can resize it and change its location on the slide. You might choose to make it the full size of the slide, or you might want to have it take up less room so your students can access the upcoming discussion question beneath the video.

▶ Trim a Video within a Google Slides Presentation

As teachers scour YouTube for videos that can be harnessed for learning, it is inevitable that they find videos that are mostly or partially useful for illustrating a topic or explaining a process. Perhaps you've found a ten-minute video that includes two minutes of the perfect explanation and eight minutes of boring introduction. Or maybe you've stumbled across the perfect video that could hook your students into a discussion, but the video ends with swear words. Whatever the scenario, teachers often find themselves needing to trim a video down to make it more accessible, appropriate, or to just get to the point. Embedding a YouTube video within a Google Slides presentation has the added benefit of allowing teachers to set the start and end time of the video. Once the video is embedded in the presentation, teachers can select the video, then click the Video Options button or right click (control + click on the Mac) the video to bring up a Video Options panel where start and end times can be controlled alongside options for muting the audio or setting the video to autoplay.

19

▶ Focus Students by Removing (Potentially Inappropriate) Distractions

YouTube has a ton of educational content, but there is some that we'd rather our students not see. Whether it is the totally inappropriate thumbnail displayed in the sidebar of suggested videos or the racist, profanity-laced comments beneath the videos, many teachers have found themselves in a situation where they needed to click away from controversial content to avoid embarrassment, a difficult parent conversation, or worse. In the event that students are subjected to something inappropriate, it's best to deal with it openly and honestly while engaging students in a conversation about being digitally resilient. Given the choice, however, most teachers would prefer to avoid this situation, and there are ways to do that. But inappropriate content isn't the only thing that can interrupt the flow of learning. Plenty of teachers have experienced capturing their students' attention and directing it to the screen at the front of the room only to be met with an advertisement instead of the chosen video. Momentum lost. Now, as long as YouTube and the creators of all its content are benefiting from advertising, a permanent solution to removing or minimizing ads is unlikely; however, a determined teacher can take these steps to stay ahead of the game:

- ▸ Embedding a video in a Google Slide deck doesn't avoid advertisements or suggested videos at the end of the video, but it does keep any ugly comments out of view of your class.

- ▸ A Google search for "block ads," "ad blocker," or similar terms will turn up plenty of options to review. Most web browsers allow for extensions or plug-ins that can block some or all advertisements. It's a bit of a moving target, and what works one day might not work the next, but it might be worth spending a bit of time finding an ad-blocking extension that works for you.

- ▸ Websites exist that can strip a YouTube video of its advertising and comments. As of this writing, viewpure.com allows users to paste a link to a video to access a page that provides the video in a pure environment stripped of any ads or comments.

YouTube is free because of advertising, and its popularity is partly due to its social engagement features, such as commenting. Teachers who attempt to avoid the downside of these two features will need to keep trying and continually learn new strategies.

▶ Flipped Teaching: Assign a Video for Homework

The concept of flipped learning or flipping the classroom relies on students accessing information at home so more time in class can be devoted to working with content. While flipping the classroom is not new to education—teachers have been assigning textbook reading as homework for ages—YouTube's explosion and popularity have made flipping even easier and, I would argue, much more effective. Given the choice between assigning a textbook chapter or a ten-minute video covering the same content, there is only one way to go: Assign the video.

The impact of homework on learning is hotly debated in education circles. Even those who argue for it recognize that its impact is minimal. But if you are going to assign homework, the least you can do is make it enjoyable. YouTube is filled with edu-tainment videos produced by channels such as V-Sauce, Crash Course, and Nat Geo. Their content is engaging. It has to be. They make their livelihood by attracting and retaining viewers, and they do this by producing high-quality content that keeps the attention of viewers with humor, pacing, and real-world connections. The real-time analytics available to producers allow them to make adjustments and tweak their products to cater to the behavior of their audience. The point is that unlike textbooks, the product is continually improving based on how users interact with it.

Spend some time searching for engaging videos that cover the same content as a chapter in your textbook. Your students will appreciate it.

▶ Embed Video in a Google Form

There are many drawbacks to homework, but homework that is not completed is especially ineffective. A video assigned as homework can be embedded in a Google form as formative assessment, and at the same time, an accountability check. Teachers can add a few questions in the form that students must answer before clicking Submit to confirm they completed the homework. The teacher's objectives and purpose of the homework should drive the type of questions being asked.

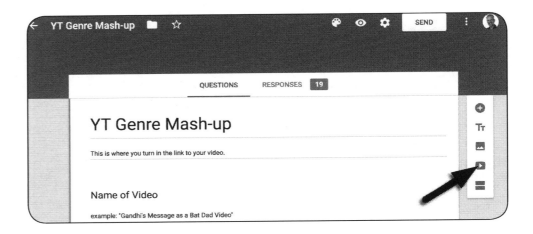

If the purpose is to introduce a new topic, then perhaps the questions should be more open-ended, such as, "Please write a five-sentence summary of your new learning" or "Describe a real-life example of the main concept that was not referenced in the video." If the purpose is to do some pre-teaching or familiarize students with new vocabulary, the questions might be a bit more specific, such as, "Describe the difference between nationalism and patriotism" or "In your own words, explain the process of photosynthesis."

If the goal is to do a more formal check for understanding, you can create a couple of fill-in-the-blank questions or multiple-choice questions. These have the added bonus of being able to be machine graded by the Google Forms Quizzes feature.

All the responses are collected in the Google form and can either be viewed in a separate spreadsheet or within the form itself. Either way, the teacher has access to all student data in one place, which makes it easy to quickly skim the responses for solid understanding and misconceptions.

▶ Create a Photo Slideshow for Parents

Parents love to see photos of their children's smiling faces. They especially love to see them smiling and laughing while learning. Taking a few minutes to create photo slideshows of what's happening in your classroom throughout the year can pay huge dividends. Nowadays, with all the different apps and software, you can have a professional looking slideshow with crossfade transitions, pan and zoom effects on each photo, and music that fits the theme completed and uploaded to YouTube within ten minutes of sitting down at your computer. And the final product will look like you spent hours producing it.

If you are using a Mac, an iPad, or even your iPhone, I suggest using iMovie to create your slideshow. It has all the editing and audio tools that you'll need, plus it has a quick upload option to YouTube. If you are on Windows, Android, or a Chromebook, you may need to look a little harder to find the perfect app or web-based option now that YouTube killed off its online editor. Of course, no matter what tools you have at your disposal, if you can use your phone to take the photos AND edit the slideshow, you're probably saving yourself some time and the headache of transferring files from device to device.

When building a photo slideshow, there are a couple tips you'll want to keep in mind: First, you'll want to limit each photo to three seconds. Don't believe me? Try watching a slideshow where a single photo stays on the screen longer than three seconds. It is pure torture. Second, stick to simple transitions between photos such as a cross-fade. Remember, the focus should be on the cute kids, not the crazy distracting visual effects. Ok, fine. If your photos are of the Valentine's Day party, then using the heart-shaped transition works, but other than that, stick to simple. Now all you need to do is share the slideshow with the parents, and (of course) I suggest using YouTube to do that.

Communicating with parents is an important component in education to-day. Many teachers use newsletters, weekly emails, blogs, and websites to keep parents informed about what their children are learning and important upcoming events. This takes time and preparation and must be prioritized within all the other tasks teachers have on their plates. If you already have an effective parent communication process in place, stick with it, but consider adding a slideshow now and again to enhance what you're already doing. If you don't currently have a parent communication plan, start off small. Set a goal of creating and sharing four slideshows throughout the year. The effort will be worth it.

▶ Allow Students to Access Information in Their Native Language with Subtitles

English-language learners can really benefit from accessing new concepts in their first language. While translating a textbook into a student's first language could be tedious and require outside assistance, information found in YouTube videos can be put into a student's language a bit more quickly—you might even say "auto-magically." With YouTube subtitles or Closed Captioning, teachers can help students to connect to important content in languages they know best.

Subtitles are not available on every YouTube video, but they are becoming more commonplace. If captions are available for a particular video, you

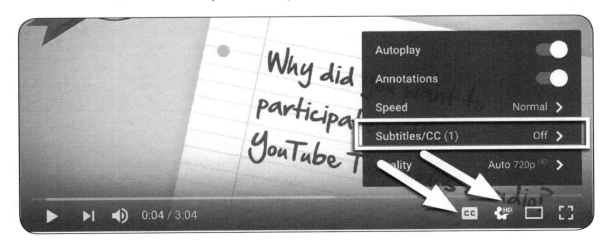

can turn them on by clicking the Subtitles/Captions icon at the bottom of the screen.

The auto-generated captions will be in the same language as the original video, but you can choose a different language by clicking Settings, which is the Gear Wheel icon. After clicking the Gear Wheel icon, choose Subtitles/CC and then Auto-Translate. From there, select the desired language from the list.

▶ Crowd Source Videos Using a Collaborative Playlist

You've searched for playlists created by other teachers, and you've created your own playlists for various purposes, but creating a playlist doesn't have to be a solo act. You can get your students or colleagues in on the fun to create collaborative playlists to which multiple people can contribute.

Contributors can add videos and also remove any they have previously added while the playlist owner maintains the rights to reorganize the list, add text annotations, and ultimately change the sharing settings.

Playlist settings

Basic   Auto add   **Collaborate**

Collaborators can add videos to this playlist
They will be listed here.

Invite collaborators to add videos by sharing a link with them   Get link

Cancel   Save

Whether you and your teaching team are looking for resources for the next unit, or you've assigned students the task of finding videos that demonstrate specific concepts discussed in class, collaborative playlists are a great way to collect those resources in one place. Becky Green, an amazing teacher I have been fortunate to learn from and work with over the years (we even co-taught a section of eighth-grade US History one year) has always required her students to teach her new things. Her Homeroom students are charged with "keeping her hip" by introducing her to popular music, media, vernacular, and memes. A collaborative playlist allows students to quickly add a pop-culture, must-watch video to the "Keep Mrs. Green Hip" playlist at the spur of the moment. This playlist is responsible for introducing Mrs. Green to the Slow-Mo Guys and Katy Perry's "Firework" song, but, more broadly, it has kept her informed of the latest trends and provided her a treasure trove of relevant videos to repurpose for hooking students into her next English lesson.

The previous examples are focused on crowd-sourcing and co-discovery of content, but collaborative playlists can also function as an efficient way to collect student video projects. As students populate the playlist, their YouTube account name is displayed next to the video they submitted, making it easy for the teacher to share the collection with the school community. Remember, there's strength in numbers, and many hands make light work, so go ahead and invite others to join you on a collaborative playlist. To get started, create a playlist, then navigate to the playlist editing screen, and under Playlist Settings choose Collaborate to access the settings and a link to share.

▶ Loop a Video When Hosting Parents in Your Classroom

Throughout the year, teachers host parents in their classrooms for various events. Whether it be parent night, parent-teacher conferences, a holiday party, or some other celebration, a video of student work or simply your students' smiling faces floating across the screen will help create just the right mood. My school has a back-to-school night where parents visit their children's classrooms. They start the evening in their child's Advisory classroom or homeroom. Parents arrive at different times and trickle in over the course of twenty minutes. Having a video of my students saying, "Hello, Mom and Dad! Welcome to my advisory," assures the parents they are in the right place and breaks the ice a bit. If I can't get my act together in time to create that video, I'll at least present a video with a still photo of each student and a group photo that can accomplish the same goals. If you are a coach conducting a pre-season meeting or post-season banquet, consider playing a highlight video. If you are an elementary teacher hosting a holiday party, maybe you've got a video of a previous class performance to play in the background. In any case, YouTube has a looping feature that will allow you to set the video to automatically repeat, freeing you up to attend to other tasks or mingle with parents.

To loop a video, once you've loaded up the video player in a browser window, you can right click (control + click on a Mac) the video to bring up a contextual menu. If you select Loop from the Menu, the video will play again and again each time it completes. To check to see that you've done this correctly, right click again and you'll see there is a check mark by the word Loop.

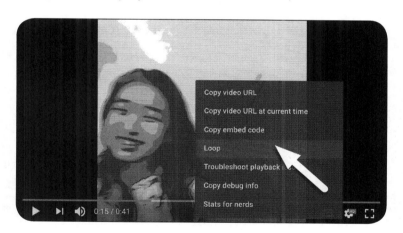

▶ Record and Edit on the Go with the YouTube App

There aren't many acceptable excuses for missing a Kodak moment anymore. With the explosion of smartphones, most of us have a high-quality camera with us at all times. So now when awesome stuff is happening around us, we don't lament that we left our expensive camera at home in a cupboard (likely with dead batteries); instead, we reach into our pocket, pull out our HD-capable phone, and start recording.

All simple camera apps on most phones have a video recording feature, and many also have direct sharing to YouTube. The YouTube app on iOS and Android super-sizes the basic camera app features in a few ways. By signing in to the YouTube app on your phone, you gain access to all your personalized preferences, such as subscriptions and playlists, but you also have a few more advanced recording options. The first option is to record a video that you can edit and upload straight to YouTube. After recording, you can trim the clip and add a filter and/or music before uploading—all within the app. The second option, which appears only after you have one hundred subscribers on your channel, is an option to go live right from the app and start broadcasting to the world. Now, you may not envision coming across many situations that need to be broadcast live, but certainly we've all been in a situation where we wished we could have recorded a teachable moment or example for our class. Can't think of why you'd ever want to record, edit, and upload on the go? Here are a couple examples:

▸ Let's say you're a science teacher, and while hiking you discover some cool rock formations. You can record yourself on location, pointing out the various types and their defining characteristics for your geology unit.

▸ Perhaps you're a language arts teacher trying to convey the importance of good grammar and spelling. With the YouTube app, you can record yourself around town in front of numerous signs with misspellings or incorrect punctuation.

▸ You have been given the opportunity to join administrators and board members on a research-and-development trip to visit innovative schools. With the YouTube app, you can report back to your colleagues and students while you're away.

▸ You're walking by a construction site on the way to work and notice three math concepts being demonstrated in the real world, so you use the app to capture them on video.

▸ While cooking at home on the weekend, you realize the recipe from which you are working illustrates a concept from your current chemistry unit. You can record it, pause it mid-playback, and ask students to predict what happens next.

- ▶ While on vacation, you visit a sculpture garden and notice it contains examples of the main points you are discussing with your senior art students, so you record a tour for the class.

- ▶ You're an online teacher facilitating a global entrepreneurship course and you want your students to get out into the field more, so you record all of your weekly videos on location at various coffee shops.

▶ Make Sub Plans as Easy as Taking a Selfie

Let's face it, sometimes it's just easier to go to work sick than to take the time to write good plans for a substitute teacher. In fact, it would probably be easier if you could just cut out the middleman, the sub, and speak directly to your students because they already have context from previous lessons, and they are familiar with your classroom procedures and expectations. Using YouTube's iOS or Android app, or even just the basic video recording in most phone camera apps, you can do just that. Here's how:

- ▶ Wake up not feeling well.

- ▶ Grab your phone off your nightstand and open the YouTube app.

- ▶ Tap the record icon and start recording with the front-facing camera.

- ▶ Hold your phone at arm's length—just like taking a selfie—and record your message, making sure to emphasize a froggy voice to be more convincing.

- ▶ Optional: leave your lights off so that the video is mostly black and very grainy.

Or maybe you'd prefer to shower, have coffee, and record your sub plans in your home office instead of the bedroom. Either way, say goodbye to those written sub plans! Just record a message to the students and send your substitute the link to show to the entire class. Alternatively, you could send the link directly to your students. Whatever the case, your students will be glad to get the info straight from you, and you'll be making it easier on the sub, who can take roll, let you do the explaining, and allow the students to do the work you've assigned. A win-win for all involved. And considering the time that you'll save recording a video rather than writing out detailed lesson plans, you'll have more time to rest and heal to get healthy and return to work.

▶ Archive Your Work

Teachers are creators. They are constantly making all sorts of new stuff including lesson plans, worksheets, posters, bulletin boards, and countless other resources. Teachers also have a reputation for being packrats. Whether they're storing manila folders in army-green file cabinets from the 1970s or in digital folders on a computer desktop, teachers like to save their creations for tweaking and future use. Some of these creations—teacher lectures, performances, classroom displays of student work, student speeches, or interactive discussions—have always proven difficult to store. YouTube provides a long-awaited solution for archiving this sort of content. It's unlimited, and free storage makes it so that you never have to think about decluttering. You can keep a copy of everything without worry about disk space. You can save years and years of classroom presentations and special events, making them available for students to view far in the future. And if you just want to store some video for your use alone, YouTube's privacy settings provide all that you need for a private file vault. You can set individual videos to private so you are the only one with access.

▶ Use Privacy Settings to Give Access Only to the Right People

One of the first questions teachers ask when they start creating and up-loading videos on YouTube is, "Who will be able to see my videos?" Maybe you are overly conscientious and don't want the world to see anything but your best work. Or maybe you have material that, for whatever reason, you want to keep from being shared widely. Perhaps you are the type of teacher who wants to share all your videos with the world, figuring sharing is caring and that if your videos help other teachers or students, you're just making the world that much better. Whatever the case, understanding the privacy settings in YouTube will give you the ability to open your content to the world, lock it down to just a few individuals, or keep it completely private and available only to you.

On YouTube, the default setting is Public, and just like it sounds, that setting makes the video viewable and searchable to the world. By changing the setting to Unlisted, you stop people from stumbling across your video or being able to search for it, but you are still able to share the link with anyone so they can view it. The Private setting limits viewing to you and anyone you invite to view that video. To invite other people, you'll need their email address.

| Basic info | Translations | Monetization | Advanced settings |

Jazz at the Cafe #sasedu

I'm testing out live streaming from mobile on YouTube while amazing #sasedu students perform some cool jazz at lunch.

✓ Public
Unlisted
Private

+ Add to playlist

Tags (e.g., albert einstein, flying pig, mashup)

With these different privacy settings, teachers can tailor YouTube to their specific needs. My suggestion is to consider going with the Public setting unless you are dealing with confidential information. Public is the least time consuming of the options and has the potential to have the widest impact by spreading your message beyond your classroom. The truth is, if you've got a great message, the world could benefit from you sharing it, and if your content isn't that great, it will be hidden among the other three hundred hours of video being uploaded each minute. What have you got to lose?

▶ Keep Students Safe with Restricted Mode

Keeping students safe while online has been a concern since the advent of the Internet, but the need has heightened with the 1:1 laptop and tablet programs adopted in schools across the globe. YouTube's Restricted Mode helps educators with this challenge by providing a filter that attempts to protect young learners from accidentally viewing inappropriate content.

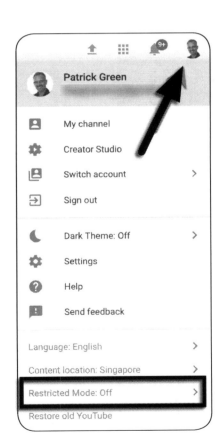

The youngest students generally won't even notice that a teacher has turned on Restricted Mode. As students grow older, it can be helpful to teach them about this feature as part of a Digital Citizenship unit and explain how they can take the initiative to block inappropriate content before they see it. In reality, a student who is determined to view questionable content will eventually find it—and likely will be looking for it in places other than YouTube—but knowing about Restricted Mode can be helpful to those not actively seeking out inappropriate material.

To enable or disable Restricted Mode, find your user icon on the right side of the YouTube page, click it and then look towards the bottom of the menu where you can toggle Restricted Mode On or Off.

▶ Provide Family-Friendly Videos for Younger Students

The YouTube Kids App is easy to use and available on both iPads and Android devices. Created with younger users in mind, it's a safer version of YouTube that includes only family-friendly videos. It is highly visual and tailored to younger users with a simplified interface and easily identifiable icons. Students who can't spell or type can still search effectively using the voice search feature. They also have the option to browse categories such as music, learning, shows, and explore on the home screen. While not an ad-free experience, all the ads have been vetted for younger audiences. The app also includes some parent controls, such as setting a timer and other such settings to tailor the experience even more.

If you are an elementary teacher in a 1:1 tablet environment, or if you have access to a few shared tablets, you might consider installing the YouTube Kids app instead of the regular YouTube app. Your students will be able to explore in a safe online environment, and you won't have to worry about them stumbling across inappropriate material.

CHAPTER FOUR

Setting Up Your Channel

If you are reading this book to learn how to create amazing content, grow your audience, and retire early off the millions you will earn from advertising, then you've got the wrong book. There are quite a few books out there dedicated to those topics, but this just isn't one of them. If you are interested in learning how to use your YouTube channel to organize your educational content to make it more accessible to students, please keep reading. Plus, there are quite a few features buried in YouTube that are super nifty for classroom teachers.

▶ Organize Your Content with a YouTube Channel

The features and tools within the YouTube Channel page give teachers a variety of ways to organize content through customizing the layout and grouping videos within sections. If you are going to take the time to create playlists or create and upload videos for your students, it makes sense to take a little extra time to organize the content on the page—the same way you would on a class blog, website, or learning management system, such as Google Classroom, Moodle, Haiku, or Schoology.

To access these more advanced features, you'll first need to enable your channel for custom layout. While you are signed in to YouTube, click on your avatar in the top right of your screen, then click on My Channel. Next, click the Edit Layout button. Find the Gear Wheel icon under your channel's art banner to access some settings where you'll be able to toggle Customize the Layout of Your Channel to On and click Save.

Customization gets a lot easier when you have completed that task because now you can move your mouse around the screen looking for the edit icon—which looks like a pencil. At this point, however, you are looking for the Add Section button at the bottom of the page. When you click it, you'll be presented with options for choosing specific content and how it should be displayed. Sections are created using a single video, one of your playlists, or a playlist created by someone else, or even a group of playlists. You might consider creating a different section for each unit or a different section for each course that you teach. Sections can be reordered easily throughout the school year if you want to always have the current topic at the top. One constraint to keep in mind as you organize the layout of your channel is that each channel has a limit of ten sections.

▶ Brand Your Channel Banner with Custom Art and Links

Even if you've spent just a short amount of time organizing your content, that big, ugly generic banner at the top of the page is likely driving you crazy. Big, ugly, generic banners say, "I don't care" and you *DO* care, so let's fix that by creating some custom channel art and links that give your channel a unique look while giving viewers an idea of who you are and what they can expect from your channel.

Links

The links are the easiest part, so we'll start there. While viewing your channel, hit the Edit Layout button. If you move your mouse to the top right of the banner, an editing icon will appear. When clicked, it reveals an option to Edit Links. By clicking on Edit Links, you'll be taken to the About section of your channel where you can add a short description of your content and add links to your social media profiles, class blog, or website. In my case, I have links to Twitter, my social bookmarks over at Diigo, and my education blog, which I update with one post a year—in a good year. Teachers using YouTube in an education context might consider providing a link to another place that students would need to go, such as the school website or the learning management system. Any links you create here can also be set to overlay on your banner.

Channel Art

Although managing links is fairly straightforward, dealing with the actual banner or channel art can be challenging and confusing for anyone who isn't skilled in creating graphics with specific dimensions. To find the details for creating your channel art, click on the Edit icon at the top right of the banner and select Add Channel Art. Look for the link at the bottom of the screen called How to Create Channel Art. If you understand what "Recommended size is 2560 X 1440 no larger than 4MB" means and have a favorite graphics editing app, you'll have all the information needed to create and upload your art.

If the instructions are confusing, I suggest putting this challenge to one of your techier students. Most likely you have a student who would be excited to help you create the banner that will be published for the entire class to see.

▶ Enable Longer Videos

YouTube's free unlimited storage is pretty awesome, but the uploaded video length is defaulted to a maximum of fifteen minutes, which can pose a problem for teachers expanding their use of the platform. The truth is, getting people to stick with a video longer than four minutes is pretty rare, so the fifteen-minute default is a good reminder to keep it short. For a teacher, however, there are a number of uses that might require uploading videos longer than fifteen minutes. Thankfully, there is a quick and easy fix to en-

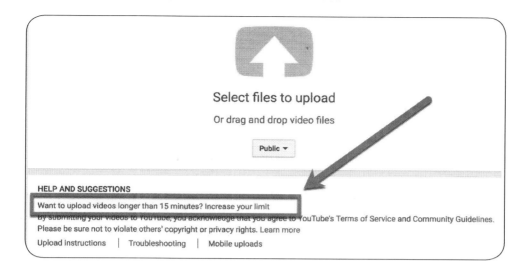

able longer videos. Just go to the upload page at YouTube.com/upload and look for the Increase Your Limit hyperlink at the bottom of the page.

You'll be led through a verification process, and when complete, you'll be able to upload videos longer than fifteen minutes. This will come in handy when you want to do any of the following:

- ▶ Record yourself teaching a lesson to submit for National Board Certification

- ▶ Record a student band, choir, or drama performance to share with parents

- ▶ Record student presentations or speeches

- ▶ Upload game footage of last night's thrilling basketball victory

▶ Make Your Channel URL Memorable for Students

As you create and publish more and more content on your channel for your students to access, you might want to make your channel easier to remember or easier to find. You can link to your channel from your school website or Learning Management System, and students can always bookmark the channel once they've accessed it for the first time, but coming up with a customized URL could be helpful and makes it easier to share. A customized URL, sometimes called a vanity URL, basically takes an ugly, randomized web address and gives it some structure that makes sense. My YouTube channel is YouTube.com/pgreensoup, which matches my other social media accounts on Twitter and Instagram. National Geographic's YouTube channel can be found at YouTube.com/natgeo. Taking time to create a customized URL doesn't mean you are vain, it just means you're a little bit geeky—and interested in making it easier for people to access your content.

There are a couple of eligibility requirements you'll need to meet, such as having one hundred subscribers. Another thing to note is you can't change a custom URL after you've chosen it, so think carefully before pulling the trigger. When you're ready, access your advanced settings by clicking your avatar in the upper right corner of YouTube, then the Settings gear wheel icon, and finally the Advanced hyperlink.

▶ Produce a Channel Trailer to Educate Students and Parents about Why You're Using YouTube

When teachers start expanding their use of YouTube and developing YouTube channels as classroom resources, it can be helpful to make sure your students and parents understand this new medium. YouTube has a couple of features—Featured Video and Channel Trailer—designed to help your audience get acquainted with your channel. Using these tools, you can designate a specific video to play automatically, depending on who is accessing your channel.

When someone visits your YouTube channel, YouTube checks to see if they are already subscribed to your channel, and if not, it serves them up a Channel Trailer. Bigtime YouTubers use the Channel Trailer to grab the attention of a first-time visitor, explain what their channel is about and what types of content it features, and ultimately build their audience by convincing the viewer to subscribe. Teachers can achieve many of those same results with a Channel Trailer that introduces who they are and how they plan to use the channel with students. It also offers a tutorial on how the content is organized for student use. The Channel Trailer essentially functions as a welcome message to students and parents. I have also found it helpful to include an appeal to students and teachers to subscribe to the channel so they can be alerted when new content is available and easily return to the channel. After you've uploaded your Channel Trailer video, go to your channel, hit the Edit Layout button and then find the For New Visitors tab and click the + Channel Trailer button.

▶ Promote a Timely Video by Featuring It on Your Channel

After students and parents become subscribers, they will no longer be greeted by the Channel Trailer when they arrive at your channel; instead, they will see a Featured Video or playlist of the teacher's choosing. This featured content is displayed in the What to Watch Next section of your channel.

When you designate the featured content, it can also be set to display as a clickable overlay that appears near the end of your other videos.

Teachers might use this tool in different ways:

- ▶ Feature a video of yourself describing the scope of learning for the current term—sort of a learning trailer for the quarter or semester
- ▶ Feature a playlist of the most recent student projects and presentations
- ▶ Feature a video that you want to promote to parents, such as a recording of a student performance
- ▶ Feature a playlist of videos covering the current unit of study
- ▶ Feature the most recent upload

After you decide what video or playlist to promote, you can access the featured content settings from your channel page by clicking the Edit Layout button, then finding the tab labeled For Returning Subscribers. To change this content in the future, return to this same place and click the pencil icon to make changes.

▶ Manage or Disable Viewer Comments

YouTube's main purpose is the storing and streaming of media, but it includes a robust set of tools for interaction that make it one of the largest social media platforms out there. Each video posted on YouTube allows viewers to interact with it via sharing options, voting it up or down—via thumbs up or thumbs down—and leaving a comment.

The commenting feature is one that requires careful thought and decision making on the part of educators. It allows for threaded conversation with the ability to vote comments up or down and has everything a teacher would want for an online discussion. It's also a public forum, which comes with obvious issues. Teachers might elect to turn the comment feature off for each video to avoid having to deal with inappropriate comments. This can be done individually as you upload each video, or you can set this as an upload default so every video you upload automatically has comments disabled.

Depending on your individual teaching situation and the purpose of your channel, you might allow comments. If this is the case, the best practice is to moderate comments, approving each one before it becomes public. This saves you from ever having to deal with an irate parent whose student was exposed to inappropriate or graphic language while accessing your channel.

Creating Content with Advanced Tools

Up to this point, we've looked at using YouTube in basic ways from creating playlists of other people's videos to using the recording feature on phones, tablets, and cameras to capture and upload your own content. As your YouTube skills grow, you can try creating videos that might require using a few third-party tools or even digging deeper into the more obscure functions found in YouTube's powerful Creator Studio. *Note: YouTube is renaming Creator Studio YouTube Studio.*

▶ Manage Content and Access Creative Tools in the Creator Studio

The Creator Studio contains powerful management, interactive, visual, and audio enhancement tools. To access the Creator Studio, make sure you are signed in to YouTube, then select your account icon and click on Creator Studio. Although this book focuses on the desktop version of Creator Studio, the YouTube Studio app on Android and iOS includes much of the same functionality.

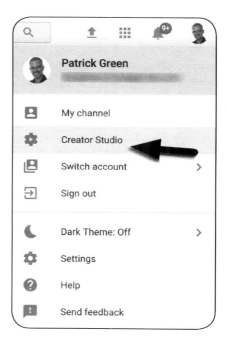

The Creator Studio can be a bit daunting, so here's a quick overview of what you'll find:

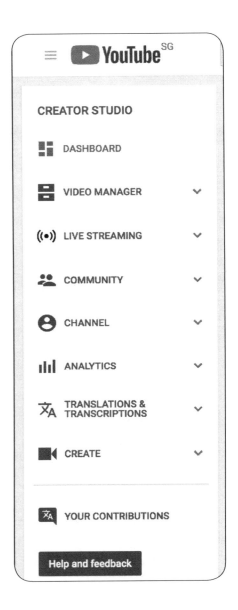

▶ Dashboard: The dashboard is the landing page of the Creator Studio. It's where you'll have a view into your most recent activity and find any updates, notifications, or tips on YouTube features.

▶ Video Manager: The video manager gives you access to all your uploaded content with tools to organize or change settings in bulk or individually. You can also edit the settings on all your playlists.

▶ Live Streaming: Tools in this section help you to create and manage live broadcasts.

▶ Community: This section allows you to view subscribers and manage comments on your videos.

▶ Channel: This section allows you to enable advanced tools for your channel such as live streaming and custom thumbnails.

▶ Analytics: The Analytics section allows you to view all sorts of data related to your videos and your channel.

▶ Create: Audio tools such as the music library are found here.

▶ Save Time by Customizing Your Default Upload Settings

Some teachers default to sharing their videos publicly, and others prefer to share them as unlisted and then distribute the link as they wish. Some teachers like to enable commenting while others prefer to disable it. Whatever the case, as you upload more videos, you'll start to develop your unique preferences. Rather than go through each individual setting every time you upload, you might consider taking time to set your default upload settings to save time in the long run. Default settings are applied to every future upload, but you can make tweaks during the upload process when necessary.

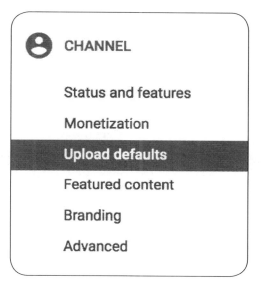

From within the Creator Studio, find Channel in the menu on the left and select Upload Defaults. You will see a number of options, and after tweaking the settings, be sure to click Save.

▶ Bring in an Expert with YouTube Live Streaming

One of the great powers of the Internet is its ability to connect people regardless of distance and geographic location. Modern classrooms still don't harness this power enough, considering that the Web allows us to interact with experts, authors, and other educators from around the world. Teachers who don't have a budget to fly in experts from halfway across the globe can use YouTube Live Streaming to video conference with these people while simultaneously streaming the session live. If your class read a novel together and really enjoyed it, consider reaching out to that author and suggesting a YouTube Live Streaming session with questions from your students. You might be surprised by the answer. After all, it is good publicity and doesn't require a flight or a hotel room—just half an hour and an Internet connection. And even if the answer is no, what do you have to lose?

Of course, if the answer is yes, you'll want to honor the author's schedule and prep your questions ahead of time. One teacher I've worked with in the past on a similar Skype-the-Author project had her students submit questions well before the session and then vote on the top ten questions. The students whose questions were selected were awarded the honor of asking their questions during the session. Don't forget to invite your classroom parents to tune-in to the broadcast. They'll want to see their child interacting with an author, but it's also a great way for you to showcase the innovative learning opportunities you are designing for your class. An added benefit is that other classrooms around the world can tune in and watch in real time while the author answers your students' questions.

Teachers have been bringing in guest speakers for years. YouTube just makes it easier and less expensive. But in many cases, you don't have to go far to find an expert. You probably have plenty of local professionals in your own community who would be willing to speak with your students about a variety of topics. The parents of your current students are a good place to start. And though they might not all be able to take a couple hours off work for take-your-dad-to-school day, they could probably find twenty minutes in their day at some point during the year to talk with your class via YouTube. You might consider publishing a list of curricular topics and having parents sign up for their areas of expertise, allowing you to schedule conversations throughout the school year. The beauty of YouTube Live Streaming is that all the conversations will be archived online, so once you have a few parents buy in, you'll have a tool for recruiting other parents in the future.

To access YouTube Live Streaming, go to your Creator Studio and then look for Live Streaming. From there, you can access all the settings.

▶ Broadcast a Classroom Event

YouTube Live Streaming can be used without the video conferencing feature. In this way, it's great for streaming live events. Think about the variety of experiences in your classroom. Which ones might be worth streaming out to interested parents? Whether your students are performing a class play, reading their poetry aloud, or performing TED-style talks, broadcasting to a wider audience can add a level of pomp and circumstance to the occasion and give students experience interacting with a larger audience. It doesn't take professional equipment. All you need is your Internet-connected laptop or tablet with a webcam and a YouTube account, and suddenly your students are performing for a world-wide audience.

If you start exploring live streaming, there are some copyright rules to consider; for example, if you are streaming a graduation ceremony and your school band plays a copyrighted piece of music as the students file in, You-Tube might flag that and shut you down, but it should be smooth sailing if everything you broadcast is a student-created original.

To access YouTube Live Streaming, go to your Creator Studio and look for Live Streaming. From there, you can access all the necessary settings.

As for privacy concerns, YouTube gives you the same options for live streaming as it does for any individual video; you can choose Unlisted, Public or Private. Depending on your school and the age of your students, you might want to consult administration or seek parental permission.

▶ Search for Copyright-Free Audio to Use Outside of YouTube

In Chapter 3, we discussed making a photo slideshow—and setting it to music—to wow your classroom parents. But the more slideshows you make, the more you'll be looking for unique music that perfectly matches the mood and theme you are trying to depict in any given slideshow. No matter what app or software you're using, the generic six or seven default music tracks will eventually get old. Thankfully, YouTube has a vast audio library of copyright-free music that is searchable by genre. The best part is that you can download the audio files to use in other creative projects or video creation applications outside of YouTube such as iMovie or Adobe Premier. Previously, when assigning students to create a video, teachers had to know of multiple free audio sites to find usable music or bend copyright rules by claiming fair use. Today, thanks to YouTube, teachers can send students to look for suitable music in the same location where they will eventually publish their creative works.

An added bonus is that the Audio Library includes sound effects that can come in handy on many student projects. From a four-second "Cat Purr" to a thirty-two-second "Urination behind Closed Door"—much more obscure yet wildly popular with middle school boys—you and your students will have all the sound files you'll ever need to bring your creative works to life.

You can search the Audio Library using keywords or filter by genre, mood, instrument, duration, and license. You can even star certain tracks and sound effects as favorites so you can easily find them again.

To get started, go to the Creator Studio, click on Create, choose Audio Library, and toggle between the two tabs of Free Music and Sound Effects.

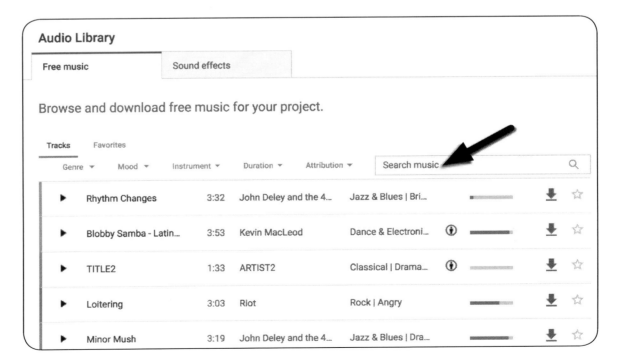

▶ Check the Usage Rights of Popular Songs

Understanding copyright law is not an easy task. For many people, fair use only muddies the waters or is used as a blanket excuse to completely ignore copyright law. In my twenty years in education, I've witnessed many instances of schools and teachers engaged in acts that are blatant copyright infringement. With adults having such difficulty with the concept, it's no wonder students receive mixed messages about copyright. Fortunately, organizations such as Creative Commons have come along and given us tools that allow us to license work in ways that allow for reuse, remixing, and sharing.

Similarly, YouTube has made changes that make the gray areas of copyright a little more black and white. In previous years, if a student uploaded a video to YouTube with a popular song as the soundtrack, YouTube would simply remove the offending video. More recently, YouTube has worked with copyright owners to allow them to decide if they will allow their music to be used on YouTube or not. And for those of us who want to use popular music such as Beyoncé's "Single Ladies" as our background track, YouTube provides a tool for us to check the wishes of the artist or copyright owner. In the Creator Studio, under Create, choose Music Policies and search by song or artist to find the current policy set by that copyright holder. In the case of "Single Ladies," the video would not be immediately taken down. It would be viewable worldwide, but the video's creator would not be able to monetize the video.

Music Policies

This directory lists songs and their current policies set by the copyright holders.

Tracks	Revenue sharing ▼	Search music 🔍
⌄ Chantaje	Shakira feat. Maluma	▬▬
⌄ Gangnam Style	Psy	▬▬
⌄ See You Again (feat. Charlie Puth)	Wiz Khalifa	▬▬

The Music Policies tool is a great way for teachers to find out if they can use popular songs in their videos, but it's even more effective in teaching copyright to students in a simple way. When students ask if they are allowed to use a popular song, teachers can respond by explaining that someone owns the copyright to the song, and there is a tool within YouTube where the copyright owners disclose whether or not they will allow it to be used in a video. Finally, some black and white in an otherwise gray area.

▶ Teach Content with a Screencast

As you search YouTube for videos related to your classes and curate content for students in playlists, you'll surely come across content that was created by other teachers. Some of this educational content is filmed on location, requiring multiple cameras and many hours of editing in a professional application. There's also plenty of content that was created by one person sitting at their laptop, recording their computer screen while narrating audio over the top. We call these screencasts. YouTube is filled with screencasts by teachers who took a few minutes to record themselves speaking over one of their slide deck presentations.

Teaching by screencasting—narrating over a slide deck—has several benefits. By uploading the video to YouTube, students can access the content at their convenience. This is particularly helpful to the student who was absent from class when the material was first presented but also to students who need to review the material. One bonus is that learning-support teachers and parents can watch how you taught a specific lesson and use it to help their struggling learner better understand the concept. A higher-level International Baccalaureate (IB) physics teacher once remarked that another benefit of screencasting is teachers can review their own screencasts the following year to brush up on more difficult concepts before teaching them again.

As flipping the classroom—teachers recording video lessons and requiring students to watch them at home—has gained popularity, screencasting has become commonplace in schools. It is highly likely you already have colleagues in your school who are familiar with screencasting, and it is even more likely you have access to the tools to do it yourself. At the most basic level, all you need is a computer with a microphone and software that can record the computer screen. Both Macs running OSX and Windows PCs running Windows 10 have built-in software that allows you to create screencasts. On Macs, you can use QuickTime Player, and on PCs, you'll need to use the Xbox app. If you are on a Chromebook (or Mac, or PC), check out Screencastify.com to access a fantastic product with plenty of screencasting power built into a Chrome extension. If you need some help getting started, there are (Yes, you guessed it!) plenty of screencast tutorials on YouTube.

When you've learned to use the software, you'll need to fire up a slide deck using PowerPoint, Keynote, or Google Slides, put it in full-screen mode, record your narration as you click through the slides, and upload the final product to YouTube.

A few more things to keep in mind as you start screencasting:

- ▶ **Screencasting is super humbling.** You'll stumble on your words, say the wrong thing, and make mistakes. Be prepared for this and don't give up. As with anything, screencasting takes a while to master. Remember, when your students are struggling with learning something new, you don't let them quit.

- ▶ **Creating a screencast in one take is nearly impossible.** If you are creating anything longer than a minute, you'll likely need to use some editing software—iMovie or Windows Movie Maker—to clean it up.

- ▶ **Advanced screencasting tools exist.** There are many free and paid screencasting apps on the market that have more functionality than the default tools that ship on your device. As you become more skilled, you might want to do an online search for "best screencasting software" to see what's currently available.

- ▶ **Learn from the pros.** There are a number of educational screencasters on YouTube who have been creating content for a long time. Channels like MathBFF have even developed their own unique style. As you are getting started, it's worth doing a little homework and checking out channels like Bozeman Science, Khan Academy, and PatrickJMT to see what's possible.

▶ Demonstrate a Piece of Software with a Screencast

In today's classroom, teachers are having students communicate their thinking and learning in so many creative ways beyond traditional essay writing. Because this often requires students to learn new digital tools or apps, it falls on the teacher to do some direct instruction around the use of new tools. In our book *Classroom Management in the Digital Age*, Heather Dowd and I encourage teachers to avoid leading students through a long series of clicks to learn a new piece of software. Keeping twenty-plus students in the same place is not just impossible, it can also be maddening for the teacher and boring for many of the students. A better approach is to do a live demo with students just watching—and not trying to keep up with the clicking—so they can get the overall concept before trying it out on their own. By providing a screencast of the direct instruction on new software or other digital tools, students can review the steps when they are ready to begin or when they get stuck—and even do it from home.

To create a screencast or how-to video that teaches multiple steps for using a piece of software, follow the same process you would use for narrating a slideshow, but instead of using slides, just record your full screen as you click through the software.

As you think about the kinds of tutorials you might want to screencast for your students, consider this list of general ideas to get the juices flowing:

- ▶ How to submit an assignment with your school's Learning Management System
- ▶ How to create a blog post and tag it appropriately
- ▶ How to use the commenting features in Google Docs when peer editing
- ▶ How to create a screencast using the built-in tools on the student devices

▶ Screencast a How-to-Use-an-App Video on a Tablet

Teachers in classrooms where students are predominately using iPads or Android tablets would benefit from being able to screencast the process of using an app. Screencasting from a tablet can be a bit trickier, but worth learning so you can better support your students with how-to videos uploaded to YouTube for anytime-and-anywhere viewing.

There are multiple ways to screencast a tablet. In fact, there are apps built specifically for screencasting that have built-in whiteboard tools for marking up documents while narrating. A search for "screen recording" or "screencast" in Apple's app store or the Google Play store will produce plenty of options. Alternatively, here are a few popular options:

iOS 11—As of Apple's iOS 11 update, iPad and iPhone users can record the device screen with a built in functionality. You'll need to enable Screen Recording by going to Settings – Control Center and then Customize Controls. Once complete, you can initiate a recording of any actions on your screen from the Control Center, which is just a quick swipe up from the bottom of the screen.

iOS 10 and earlier—If you want to screencast your actions on an iPad or iPhone with an OS prior to 11, connect it to your Mac via the USB to lightning cable and use Quicktime as you would to record your Mac's screen. The only difference is you'll need to select the iPad or iPhone as the device to record. When you've connected the devices with a lightning cable, open Quicktime on the Mac and go to File and New Movie Recording. Using the drop-down arrow next to the Record button, select the iPad under Camera instead of the built-in camera on your Mac. The recording view will change to whatever is on your iPad. You can hit the Record button and start tapping and talking. When you are finished, upload to YouTube.

Android—YouTube makes it really easy to screencast on an Android device using the YouTube Gaming app. The app was created to record and live stream game play but works great for recording any activity on your screen without the need for a second device. A bonus feature is the ability to use the front-facing camera simultaneously so students can watch your onscreen actions while seeing your smiling face and hearing your voice. Check out YouTube for specific how-to instructions via screencast, of course.

▶ Provide Feedback on a Student Assignment with a Screencast

Have you ever hauled a pile of papers home for the weekend to grade? Stopping to think about whether students would actually read your comments probably wouldn't improve your outlook in that moment. We've all experienced students who look past all the markup just to find the final grade before tossing the assignment in the trash. In my experience, students are much more likely to act on my feedback if I conference with them rather than hand them back a paper covered in red ink. As valuable as conferencing with students is, it is difficult to make time in class to meet individually with twenty-plus students.

Screencasts offer a way to give students feedback in a way that might be more useful to them than written comments. As a teacher, you might even find you save time giving students feedback via a ninety-second screencast than you would by writing it all down. And if your students are like mine, they'll be glad to not have to try to decipher your chicken scratch. To try this method, read through the student's work, then fire up your screencasting software, pop open the student work on your screen, and begin recording your thoughts as you scroll through the work. You can use the cursor to highlight the specific text to which you're referring as you speak.

> The video screencast was perceived by students as the teacher actively helping them to improve rather than as judging them with a grade and editing marks.

Teachers who have tried this method remarked that it changed the way students received the information. The video screencast was perceived by students as the teacher actively helping them to improve rather than as judging them with a grade and editing marks. The act of screencasting does inevitably change the type of feedback teachers give, as the conference-like approach leads to more talk about conceptual changes and strategies rather than a focus on writing errors.

The first time you try it, you might take longer than normal to provide feed-back. But if students end up doing more with the feedback by making a plan to improve their writing, the time will be well spent, and you'll be faster on your second go-round.

▶ Link to Other Important Info with Cards and End Screens

YouTube offers video creators the ability to layer additional information over their videos with the use of the Cards feature and the End Screens feature. Cards were designed to allow users to add clickable information such as a link to another video, playlist, or outside website at any time dur-ing the video, while End Screens are designed (as the name suggests) to be displayed at the end of a video. Teachers can harness these features to give students contextual information they might need. Let's say a social studies teacher created a four-minute screencast on a topic but finds out many students are having trouble understanding the topic because they don't have a grasp of the vocabulary used. Rather than scrap the video, the teacher creates a new video reviewing the necessary vocabulary and creates a card that pops up in the original video to direct students to the vocabulary video if they need it. A science teacher who records a video on a concept from unit three can feel free to reference foundational material from unit one without going into detail. She simply creates a card with a link to a playlist of the previous unit's videos that might be necessary for some students to review.

Another example is an elementary teacher who records monthly videos previewing upcoming learning and events as a way to communicate with parents and build excitement among students. In each video she referenc-es her class website, where parents can find more detailed information and updates. She creates a card, which is timed to display when she references the website, that allows viewers to click directly to the site. She can also use an End Screen to share the link with her audience at the end of the video as she wraps things up and summarizes her message.

At the time of this writing, Cards and End Screens are relatively new features that YouTube continues to enhance, so I won't go into detail on the specifics. In general, Cards and End Screens are accessed from within the editing view of a specific video that a user has already uploaded. Go to the Creator Studio to find the video you'd like to edit and click on the Edit button to get to an editing screen. There you'll find functions including tabs for Cards and End Screens.

▶ Attract More Student Clicks with Custom Thumbnails

A video thumbnail is the still image that represents the video in Google search results or when browsing YouTube. It's a snapshot that displays alongside the title of the video.

Five Boys Four-Wheeling
Patrick Green
48 views · 1 year ago

Out with October, in with Movember
Patrick Green
172 views · 1 year ago

Table of Contents Automatically in Word Mac 2011
Patrick Green
340 views · 1 year ago

Workout Machine
Patrick Green
186 views · 2 years ago

We all know that you shouldn't judge a book by its cover, but thumbnails, just like book covers, do a lot to attract attention. If you're a teacher who is regularly screen-casting and producing video content for your students, or you've spent time customizing your channel and organizing your content, you'll probably want to take the next step and add custom thumbnails to each video to draw more students to your channel. Analytics suggest you'll get more students to watch your video if you've spent time creating an attractive thumbnail.

By default, YouTube gives you a choice of three still images that it auto-generates from your video to use as the thumbnail. The thumbnail options are presented when you upload a video and can be accessed for any previously uploaded video by clicking Edit from the Video Manager page.

To enable custom thumbnails, you'll need to verify your YouTube account if you haven't already. Go to YouTube.com/verify to be led through the necessary steps. Upon completion, click the Custom Thumbnail button available beneath the three auto-generated options to choose and upload a custom thumbnail from your desktop.

You can make a custom thumbnail in any graphics application or application capable of exporting a graphic. If you're a Photoshop expert, you're ready to go! PowerPoint, Keynote on a Mac, or Google Presentations all work equally well. You just need to create a file with the correct dimensions and save it as an image file. If the specifications below don't make sense to you, I suggest asking one of your techy students—they'll be honored to help you get started.

- ▶ Resolution should be 1280 x 720
- ▶ Aspect Ratio: 16:9
- ▶ Acceptable image formats: .JPG, .GIF, .BMP, or .PNG.
- ▶ File Size Limit: under 2MB

Empower Students to Create

YouTube is a powerful creative tool with many hidden functions that can be harnessed for learning, and there's no reason all of YouTube's creative and organizational tools should be reserved for adults. In this section we will explore using some specific strategies to empower the students in your classroom. At this point, it might be helpful to review the previous sections of this book with an eye towards putting YouTube in the hands of students so they can demonstrate their learning.

▶ Students Reflect on Their Learning Via Video

We are teaching a YouTube generation. Our students are much more comfortable recording videos of themselves than we are. When asking students to reflect on a product or a process, assigning a video instead of a written response has many benefits. Students perceive video to have high expectations for communication, but they see writing as high expectations for product. In some instances, where a student can record a quality video in a few minutes, they might spend much more time writing and then editing the same reflection on paper. Many students are more comfortable with spoken language than written language, and a video offers a medium where they are better able to "show" what they mean. Teachers who have used video reflections with their students have reported that students share more information and more critical and honest feedback. Sometimes it is easier to say things than write them down—particularly when it comes to issues in which tone might be misinterpreted; for example, a student is more likely to try to explain a sensitive partnership issue that arises during a collaborative project through a video reflection because they can massage the message much better than they can in writing.

When attempting this the first time, consider giving students a time limit of one or two minutes. Remember, you'll have to watch all of them. It might also be helpful to have a bulleted list of three prompts or questions you want students to answer. Lastly, consider collecting the video reflections by using a collaborative playlist. You can easily share the link to the collaborative playlist via email or post it on your learning management system or class website. The playlist will make for an easier viewing experience because all the video reflections will play continuously, one after the other, without requiring you to open up separate files.

▶ Students Self-Assess a Live Performance

Communication is important. Whether you label it a twenty-first century skill, a career and college readiness skill, or a desired student learning outcome, most schools have communication on their list of cross-curricular skills that are the responsibility of all teachers. This is why many teachers from almost every discipline offer opportunities for students to present in front of the class through public speaking or some other practice.

Most teachers assess the student presentation live, and some teachers allow for peer assessment. A common missing component, however, is self-assessment because students obviously cannot simultaneously be a performer and a member of the audience. Video solves this problem. By recording student presentations and allowing students to self-assess, students will be able to compare their own observations to the teacher's evaluation and peer feedback.

In today's classroom, whether every student has an individual device, or there's only one shared desktop or laptop, recording and sharing video is easy. As every school and classroom context is different, here are two examples to help you apply this concept to your own classroom:

A high school drama teacher uses a video camera to record each of the in-class small group student performances. She stops the recording after each group so each performance can be uploaded to YouTube separately. After class, she uploads the recordings to her YouTube channel for students to access. Students create a blog post on their school blog where they embed their performance and write a response to a series of prompts.

A middle school language arts teacher in a 1:1 laptop classroom requires her students to present an oral book report. Taking turns, the students place their laptops on the front desk and stand facing the screen so they can use the laptop's webcam to record themselves. The teacher requires that students upload their performance to their individual YouTube channels as part of their portfolio of work. For homework, students assess their own performance on the same rubric that the teacher uses.

▶ Recapture and Repurpose Class Time with Recorded Presentations

Opportunities for students to present in front of their peers are extremely valuable and won't be tossed out of the teacher tool kit anytime soon. The main drawback, though, is the time it takes to get through an entire class of presentations. Effective teachers try to engage all students during presentations with active listening activities or require students to peer assess each performance with a goal of making each presentation a learning opportunity for all. But even for the most engaging of student presentations, this can turn into a long, monotonous slog; for example, Scott Hall has five fifty-minute sections of eighth-grade US history each day with twenty-five students in each section. With that load, which is typical for a middle school teacher, it can take almost an entire week to get through all the presentations. And while peer assessment and learning from other students is valuable, one might wonder about the diminishing returns on the fourth straight day of presentations. So how can Scott save time while still giving every student the opportunity to present? Again, video is the answer.

Recording student presentations for assessment is not that difficult to organize. If you are already recording student presentations for self-assessment, as in the previous strategy, you've got the technical bits down. All you need are multiple presentation spaces so two or three students can present at the same time without being in the same room. After all, teachers should be able to assess student performance consistently, whether it's live or recorded. Let's play out a couple of scenarios where all students have an opportunity to present live and all students have an opportunity to provide feedback to other students:

An elementary teacher divides her fourth graders into four groups. She has invited three volunteer parents to join her for the day, assigning one adult to each of the groups. The groups break into the four corners of the room where each student delivers a presentation to their group. The students are used to a busy classroom and various stations and activities happening simultaneously, so they are not distracted by what is going on in the other three corners of the room. The adults at each station record and upload the videos to YouTube so the students can add the presentation to their portfolio for parent conferences.

A seventh-grade math teacher in a 1:1 laptop program has students design games at the end of the probability unit of study. Each student creates a presentation detailing how the game is played, the math behind it, and how the game would, theoretically, make a profit. To save class time, students record their presentations at home with at least one audience member (typically a parent) and upload the videos to YouTube. The students are put into groups of five and required to peer assess the other four group members' videos during class the next day. Students start class by using their laptops to watch one another's videos, which only takes one day, leaving another day to actually play the games.

A high school chemistry teacher divides his class into three groups. The students in each group are responsible for assessing each of their group members' presentations. The teacher schedules two bookable collaborative spaces in the library, allowing all three groups to present at once. Because the students are older and more responsible, and the teacher has developed a culture of trust in his classroom, he is not concerned about behavior issues. He assesses one group's presentations live while viewing the other two groups outside of class via their YouTube submissions.

In each of these scenarios, teachers could save multiple hours of class time—and repurpose it for other activities—while still addressing the required learning targets. Additionally, the students in these scenarios suffered less peer assessment fatigue (that's a real thing; I've seen it) and likely were more focused and able to offer more constructive feedback to their classmates.

▶ Students Create an Authentic Portfolio

Students being able to see their growth over time is a powerful concept allowing students and teachers to set goals and determine next steps for the learner. Online portfolios are often heralded at education conferences, yet are seemingly rarely implemented with fidelity in schools. Clunky portfolio software, lack of teacher buy-in, student perception, and portability issues might be responsible for numerous portfolio implementation dips in schools around the world. YouTube, based on its popularity and versatility, might just be the perfect digital portfolio tool that could last. First, YouTube is an authentic and popular tool that students want to use and are already using without teacher direction. Goodbye, student ownership issues! Students of all ages are already out there uploading their creative work to YouTube, and many are invested in increasing likes and subscribers, which is authentic feedback. Second, YouTube is the farthest thing from clunky, with unlimited storage, integration with hundreds of apps, and accessibility on every major operating system and device. Portability issues evaporate with all videos stored in the cloud and accessible anytime, anywhere. Third, video is so versatile that any task, product, or performance where students demonstrate their skills or knowledge can be stored as video. Performance, speech, presentation—record and upload. Essay? The student could screencast it or record themselves reading it. Diorama? (Please, not another diorama.) Students could record themselves giving a close-up description of all the components. Once it is common practice for students to upload final products or process pieces to YouTube, they'll want to move on to curating, organizing, and personalizing their channel to tell the story of their growth. Imagine having access to digital video portfolios of every student before you begin teaching them. How might that change your practice and processes?

▶ Students Record Themselves Reading

One specific example of a performance task that absolutely should be captured and curated in a student portfolio is video of the student reading. For young learners, the growth that can be seen over the first couple years of elementary school is enormous, and archiving this footage is excellent for so many purposes, such as student goal setting or use at parent teacher conferences.

Students using webcams to record themselves reading is also valuable for older students, even those in high school. Technically, recording with a webcam—on a phone or tablet—is still the same, but the purpose changes slightly. Older students can benefit by recording themselves reading their own writing and then reviewing it by listening to themselves read. Many students can find more areas for improvement in their writing when they listen to it read aloud than if they were simply editing on paper.

▶ Students Record Rough Drafts of Their Presentations

Similar to finding errors in their written work, students can benefit from watching themselves give a speech or make a presentation. While a teacher might not want to devote class time to this task, it's extremely helpful for students to have uploaded a video of an at-home rough draft of their presentation before the actual in-class presentation. You could take it a step further by asking students to use the presentation rubric to self-assess their rough drafts before doing the live presentation. In many cases, the teacher would never watch the rough draft, but it might prove useful in some situations.

▶ Provide Students with Actionable Feedback Via YouTube Comments

Typically, when teachers assess student work, a rubric is involved. Likewise, specific criteria or protocols are provided for students when peer or self-assessment is part of the learning process. Whether referencing categories from a rubric or using some other protocol, teachers can utilize YouTube's commenting feature as the place to collect all the feedback. If students are submitting projects through YouTube, it makes sense that the feedback be hosted in the same place, staying attached to the product. By posting the feedback as a YouTube comment, you might find students are more likely to read and then make use of the feedback. This strategy might be even more powerful when used as part of the learning process rather than on a summative assessment; for example, a teacher might ask students to record a rough draft of their presentations and direct students to leave feedback for one another according to a specific criterion. The students will then use that feedback to improve their presentations before the final performance.

▶ Students Submit Video Evidence Meeting Criteria of a Performance Task

While a stack of worksheets might be a slog for a teacher to grade, it is often much easier and less daunting than completing collaborative, interactive, and authentic performance-based assessments. The worksheets are simple to grade in that answers to questions are more or less right or wrong and can be scored accordingly, and each worksheet is identical, allowing the teacher to get into a groove while cranking out scores in one sitting. When a teacher attempts to grade twenty-plus students during a live, authentic, interactive activity, it can be much more complex, making management and accurate assessment nearly impossible. It can be especially unfair to the student who performs perfectly when the teacher's attention is devoted to another area of the classroom. While many teachers might just avoid the difficulty by sticking with worksheets, Matt Findlay, an expert teacher at the International School of Prague, solved this conundrum in his classroom by having students submit video evidence of themselves meeting the criteria of a performance assessment. Literature circles in an English or language arts classroom are a common scenario where this strategy could be applied.

Let's say you've given students the option to choose from among five books and then divided the class into groups based on their choices so all members of the group are reading the same book. You've asked them to read a specific portion of the book and come to class prepared to engage in a literature circle. The students are aware of your expectations for inter-action and they know you are looking for them to do the following:

- ▸ Ask a question
- ▸ Listen actively
- ▸ Respond to questions posed by others
- ▸ Refer to the text
- ▸ Make a connection (to personal life or another book)

Instead of running around the classroom trying to catch students meeting the criteria while your back is turned to other students, have all the students set their laptops or tablets in front of them and use their webcams to record themselves interacting in the literature circle. If you are doing this for the first time, you might need to remind students they are essentially ignoring their devices for the duration of the assessment, looking over the tops of them so they can fully interact with their group members. When the literature circle is complete, students review their footage, which only includes themselves, cutting out examples of their participation and splic-ing it together with titles describing the criteria so you know exactly what each example is supposed to show. A final product would be a three-min-ute highlight reel of a student's participation that is uploaded to YouTube for the teacher to view and assess.

You can see how this strategy makes assessment of a live performance much more manageable. It would take the teacher only three minutes to assess each student. Of course, a teacher can save even more time by embedding himself in one of the groups, allowing him to assess that group live and thus reducing the number of videos to watch after class. There are benefits for students too. It helps kids to reflect on their own performance. They get an instant replay of their contributions, allowing them to see what they're doing well and what they need to work on.

Matt Findlay's 3 #ProTips for Implementation

▶ To avoid distraction, I suggest kids turn their screen brightness down all the way. The video will still record, but they seem less tempted to pull faces at themselves.

▶ I also tell them I don't really care about the video quality, but it's helpful if their faces are on screen. When editing, they can skim through the video and grab clips where they see their lips moving. Then they can select the best of those clips for their highlight reel.

▶ Sometimes you might need to use a "big brother" element. A few kids thought the highlight reel approach meant they could say one or two intelligent things and then screw around the rest of the time. To head that off, I let them know I might collect one full video from a group and spot check it to see if everyone was behaving constructively. That's also an option if kids complain about disruptive or disrespectful behavior in a given group. I don't find that I need to do that very often, however.

▶ Students Make a Movie

Every educator who ever asks students to make a movie as an assignment needs to have tried it first so they have an understanding of the time and the skills required. There are so many components: scripting, storyboarding, and shot selection, just to name a few. There are also a bunch of technical elements including lighting and sound that cannot be ignored. And once the shots have been captured, there are multiple hours of editing necessary to complete to project. Asking students to make a movie is a worthy, creative task that teachers should have in their arsenal, but it is important to acknowledge the scaffolding that might be required. The first time you try it, you might want to build in a buffer; it's likely to take students longer than you think.

Depending on your classroom context, you might have access to a few video cameras, or perhaps every student has an iPad or a laptop. MacBooks, iPads, and PCs all ship with movie editing software and have professional-level software options, such as Final Cut Pro and Adobe Premier. Chromebooks, on the other hand, have far fewer options with YouTube having killed its online video editor in the fall of 2017. WeVideo is one online video editing option currently available. Stay tuned to youtube.com/pgreensoup, as I'll be sure to make a video announcement when there is another option for Chromebooks.

▶ Students Make Thinking Visible with a Screencast

We want our students to be able to solve problems, but often teachers want more than just the right answer—they want to know how students arrived at the right answer. Understanding students' thinking or the process they used to solve a problem allows teachers to better understand the learning that is taking place. As a student, I hated being told, "Show your work!" As an adult, I now understand the value to the teacher. Screencasting is a great way for students to make their thinking visible. Here are two examples of what this might look like in a classroom:

For his sixth-grade Egyptian museum project, Emilio chose to create his Egyptian Pyramids in Minecraft rather than use paper-mache. Instead of submitting his Minecraft world to a teacher who has never navigated the game, Emilio used his laptop to create a screencast tour that he submitted via YouTube. Emilio recorded his screen as he flew through his world, pointing out important aspects through narration as he explained his choices and creative process.

In her seventh-grade math class, Elena is used to working out problems with a stylus and a simple drawing app on her iPad. Occasionally her teacher asks her to switch over to a screencasting app to record her process while she narrates her thinking simultaneously. These screencasts are uploaded to YouTube as formative assessments.

▶ Assign YouTube Genre Mash-ups as Creative Tasks

A common instructional strategy that teachers of many subjects have used to engage students in higher-order thinking is to assign the creation of an original product or performance. A quick search of the Internet will produce a lengthy list of possibilities such as skits, newscasts, songs, raps, and weather reports. The thinking behind this strategy is that students will come to understand the content more deeply by having to apply or transfer knowledge in a new way. Here is an example of how this might look in an eighth-grade social studies classroom using a jigsaw format:

Twenty-six students are divided into six groups. Each group is assigned a different event from the American Revolution unit. All groups are tasked with creating a newscast and performing it in front of the class.

This type of scenario is commonplace in many schools and has been for many years, so where does YouTube come in? There are two ways YouTube can add value here: First, by recording and uploading the students' performances, teachers can archive exemplars and allow for reflection and inclusion in student portfolios—not to mention catch the next viral video on camera or simply share it with parents. Second—and this one is powerful—YouTube has a new generation of genres that can be assigned to students. If you apply the term loosely, you will see that YouTube is full of them and helping create new ones all the time. Imagine asking students during the Egypt unit to demonstrate their knowledge of mummification as a product review video. What about having students describe the parts of an atom as a workout video? How about the causes of the Civil War as an "Annoying Orange" video or photosynthesis in the genre of an "unboxing" video? A newscast is fun, but I suspect kids might be slightly more engaged in doing The Boston Tea Party as a Bat Dad video. The possibilities are endless, and so might be the hilarity that ensues.

If you want to spice up this strategy a bit more, here are two suggestions: First, try adding some randomness to the mix by having the topics and genres assigned and matched up live in front of the students with a push of a button. You can download the YouTube Genre Mash-up Generator spreadsheet at YouTubeClassroom.com, which is already set up to randomly pair your topics with the genres you choose.

The second suggestion is to require students to have their final take uploaded to YouTube by the end of the class period. You could even use a collaborative playlist to collect the submissions. Constraints can inspire creativity, and by establishing the deadline as the end of the class time, you are helping students focus and be productive. After all, you aren't looking for a completely polished video here; you are looking for students to be engaged in the higher-order thinking that comes with application and transfer.

▶ Teach Students to Be Digitally Resilient through Managing Comments

Many teachers encourage students to publish online through blogs or websites because it is more authentic than having their teacher as the only audience. By asking students to publish completed works online, teachers have a venue where they can instruct and guide students in creating a positive digital footprint and practicing respectful communication through commenting on one another's work. Teachers who engage students in online interaction often have lessons built around commenting, such as the elements of a good comment and the proper response to an inappropriate comment. The best practice is to teach students to moderate comments so only approved comments go public.

Students are much more likely to have to deal with an ugly comment on YouTube than on their blog simply because of YouTube's more public nature. But that doesn't mean we should discourage our students' use of YouTube. On the contrary, we should be engaging them in publishing their work to the world and guiding and supporting them along the way. There is no denying that likes and comments carry a lot of weight with students. From curating the perfect set of photos on Instagram to creating skateboarding highlight reels on YouTube, they are already engaged in sharing their lives with an online audience, often without adult guidance. Unfortunately, mean people exist, and our students are going to be exposed to them. By encouraging students to use YouTube, we have the opportunity to help them develop digital resilience and the skills to deal with other people's bad behavior.

Depending on the developmental level of the learners, consider the following teaching points:

- ▶ Always moderate comments. Never allow comments to post automatically.

- ▶ Any comment that makes you uncomfortable should be reported to an adult so the adult can assist with next steps, such as documentation or deletion and further follow up.

- ▶ Block and report users who leave inappropriate comments.

- ▶ Ignore and delete.

You also might want to consider creating student guidelines for online sharing like the ones that Heather Dowd and I included in *Classroom Management in the Digital Age.*

Online Sharing Guidelines from
Classroom Management in the Digital Age

Why share online?

- ▸ To practice creating work for an audience beyond the classroom walls
- ▸ To connect and collaborate with peers and experts globally
- ▸ To archive your learning in one place and reflect on your growth
- ▸ To showcase your creativity and share your ideas

What you post online is permanent. Use the following to help you decide what is appropriate to publish.

- ▸ Think before you post. Ask yourself . . .
- ▸ Is this something I want the world to see?
- ▸ Would sharing this offend anyone?
- ▸ Would I want this to represent my abilities?
- ▸ Treat other people the way you want to be treated. Ask yourself . . .
- ▸ Would I say this to someone in person?
- ▸ How would I feel if someone said this to me?
- ▸ Do not share personal information such as last name, address, phone number, or email address.
- ▸ Properly cite media used from another source. Ask yourself . . .
- ▸ Who is the original creator of this work?
- ▸ Do I have permission to use this work?

▶ Teach Students about Copyright and Fair Use

As you incorporate YouTube into your lessons, and students begin to create and upload more content, issues of copyright will arise, and students might have direct questions about it. These are excellent opportunities to harness a teachable moment. Beyond its amazing tools, YouTube provides some helpful documentation of copyright and fair use for teachers to utilize. You can find YouTube's copyright resources at YouTube.com/yt/copyright.

▶ Final Tip: Inspire Others by Sharing Your Creative Uses of YouTube

The title of this book is *50 Ways to Use YouTube in the Classroom*, yet we are way beyond 50 at this point. I didn't let the title of the book limit me to just fifty ways, and you shouldn't be limited by numbers either. As YouTube adds functionality, and as creative teachers continue to find innovative ways to enhance student learning, we should be able to continue to find new ways to harness this authentic creative tool. That's the beauty of using a tool that wasn't built for education—there isn't a manual, so we are only limited by our own creativity. Maybe you are already using YouTube in a way that wasn't shared in this book, or maybe something you read inspired you to come up with a new idea. Making a YouTube video describing your strategy is an obvious route to take, but you could also write a blog post or craft a short tweet. In any case, don't keep your creativity to yourself. Take the opportunity to inspire other teachers and build our collective repertoire by sharing your strategy with the hashtag #YouTubeClassroom.

Acknowledgments

I would like to express gratitude and thanks to the following people and organizations that have been instrumental in helping me to complete this process.

First, to my amazingly talented, creative and patient wife who allowed me to spend countless Saturday mornings creating this work.

To the fantastic educators I've had the chance to work with and learn from. So many of the ideas in this book were born out of collaborative conversations with other innovative educators at Singapore American School, International School of Prague and people I've met at education conferences around the globe and online through my PLN.

To TechSmith for creating Snagit, which I used for all of the screenshots in the book.

To the good people over at Screencastify who not only make an excellent screencasting extension for the Chrome browser, but who also have a tool for generating the dynamic QR codes used throughout this book.

More Books From EdTechTeam Press

edtechteam.com/books

The HyperDoc Handbook
Digital Lesson Design Using Google Apps

By Lisa Highfill, Kelly Hilton, and Sarah Landis

The HyperDoc Handbook is a practical reference guide for all K–12 educators who want to transform their teaching into blended-learning environments. The HyperDoc Handbook is a bestselling book that strikes the perfect balance between pedagogy and how-to tips while also providing ready-to-use lesson plans to get you started with HyperDocs right away.

Innovate with iPad
Lessons to Transform Learning

By Karen Lirenman and Kristen Wideen

Written by two primary teachers, this book provides a complete selection of clearly explained, engaging, open-ended lessons to change the way you use iPad with students at home or in the classroom. It features downloadable task cards, student-created examples, and extension ideas to use with your students. Whether you have access to one iPad for your entire class or one for each student, these lessons will help you transform learning in your classroom.

The Space
A Guide for Educators
By Rebecca Louise Hare and Robert Dillon

The Space supports the conversation around revolution happening in education today concerning the reshaping of school spaces. This book goes well beyond the ideas for learning-space design that focuses on Pinterest-perfect classrooms and instead discusses real and practical ways to design learning spaces that support and drive learning.

A Learner's Paradise
How New Zealand Is Reimagining Education
By Richard Wells

What if teachers were truly trusted to run education? In A Learner's Paradise, Richard Wells outlines New Zealand's forward-thinking education system in which teachers are empowered to do exactly that. With no prescribed curriculum, teachers and students work together to create individualized learning plans—all the way through the high school level. From this guidebook, you'll learn how New Zealand is reimagining education and setting an example for innovative educators, parents, and school districts to follow.

Classroom Management in the Digital Age
Effective Practices for Technology-Rich
Learning Spaces
By Patrick Green and Heather Dowd

Classroom Management in the Digital Age helps guide and support teachers through the new landscape of device-rich classrooms. It provides practical strategies to novice and expert educators alike who want to maximize learning and minimize distraction. Learn how to keep up with the times while limiting time wasters and senseless screen-staring time.

The Google Apps Guidebook
Lessons, Activities, and Projects Created by
Students for Teachers

By Kern Kelley and the Tech Sherpas

The Google Apps Guidebook is filled with great ideas for the classroom from the voice of the students themselves. Each chapter introduces an engaging project that teaches students (and teachers) how to use one of Google's powerful tools. Projects are differentiated for a variety of age ranges and can be adapted for most content areas.

Dive into Inquiry
Amplify Learning and Empower Student Voice

By Trevor MacKenzie

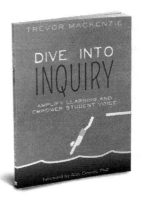

Dive into Inquiry beautifully marries the voice and choice of inquiry with the structure and support required to optimize learning. With *Dive into Inquiry* you'll gain an understanding of how to best support your learners as they shift from a traditional learning model into the inquiry classroom where student agency is fostered and celebrated each and every day.

Sketchnotes for Educators
100 Inspiring Illustrations for Lifelong Learners

By Sylvia Duckworth

Sketchnotes for Educators contains 100 of Sylvia Duckworth's most popular sketchnotes, with links to the original downloads that can be used in class or shared with colleagues. Interspersed throughout the book are reflections from Sylvia about what motivated her to create the drawings as well as commentary from many of the educators whose work inspired her sketchnotes.

Code in Every Class
How All Educators Can Teach Programming
By Kevin Brookhouser and Ria Megnin

In *Code in Every Class*, Kevin Brookhouser and Ria Megnin explain why computer science is critical to your students' future success. With lesson ideas and step-by-step instruction, they show you how to take tech education into your own hands and open a world of opportunities to your students. And here's the best news: You *don't* have to be a computer genius to teach the basics of coding.

Making Your School Something Special
Enhance Learning, Build Confidence, and Foster Success at Every Level
By Rushton Hurley

In *Making Your School Something Special*, educator and international speaker Rushton Hurley explores the mindsets, activities, and technology that make for great learning. You'll learn how to create strong learning activities and make your school a place where students and teachers alike want to be—because it's where they feel energized, inspired and *special*.

The Google Cardboard Book
Explore, Engage, and Educate with Virtual Reality
An EdTechTeam Collaboration

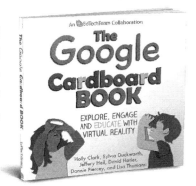

In *The Google Cardboard Book*, EdTechTeam trainers and leaders offer step-by-step instructions on how to use virtual reality technology in your classroom—no matter what subject you teach. You'll learn what tools you need (and how affordable they can be), which apps to start with, and how to view, capture, and share 360° videos and images.

Transforming Libraries
A Toolkit for Innovators, Makers, and Seekers
By Ron Starker

In the Digital Age, it's more important than ever for libraries to evolve into gathering points for collaboration, spaces for innovation, and places where authentic learning occurs. In *Transforming Libraries*, Ron Starker reveals ways to make libraries makerspaces, innovation centers, community commons, and learning design studios that engage multiple forms of intelligence.

Intention
Critical Creativity in the Classroom
By Amy Burvall and Dan Ryder

Inspiring and exploring creativity opens pathways for students to use creative expression to demonstrate content knowledge, critical thinking, and the problem solving that will serve them best no matter what their futures may bring. *Intention* offers a collection of ideas, activities, and reasons for bringing creativity to every lesson.

Making Your Teaching Something Special
50 Simple Ways to Become a Better Teacher
By Rushton Hurley

In the second book in his series, Rushton Hurley highlights key areas of teaching that play a part in shaping your success as an educator. Whether you are finding your way as a brand new teacher or are a seasoned teacher who is looking for some powerful ideas, this book offers inspiration and practical advice to help you make this year your best yet.

The Google Infused Classroom
A Guidebook to Making Thinking Visible and Amplifying Student Voice
By Holly Clark and Tanya Avrith

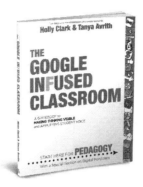

This beautifully designed book offers guidance on using technology to design instruction that allows students to show their thinking, demonstrate their learning, and share their work (and voices!) with authentic audiences. *The Google Infused Classroom* will equip you to empower your students to use technology in meaningful ways that prepare them for the future.

The Conference Companion
Sketchnotes, Doodles, and Creative Play for Teaching and Learning
By Becky Green

Wherever you are learning, whatever your doodle comfort level, this jovial notebook is your buddy. Grab a pencil, pen, crayon, or quill. Sketchnotes, doodles, and creative play await both you and your students. Part workshop, part journal, and part sketchbook, these simple and light-hearted scaffolds and lessons will transform your listening and learning experiences while providing creative inspiration for your classroom.

Bring the World to Your Classroom
Using Google Geo Tools
By Kelly Kermode and Kim Randall

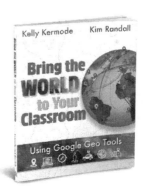

We live and work in a global society, but many students have only a very small community or neighborhood as their frame of reference. Expand their horizons and help them increase their understanding of how they fit in the global landscape using Google Geo Tools. This book is packed full of how-tos and sample projects to get you and your learners moving forward with mapping, exploring, and making connections to the world around you.

Want more YouTube in the Classroom Tips?

Here are ways to stay connected:

1. **Host a Workshop at Your School**

   ▶ **Curation to Creation: The YouTube Master's Class**—With 300 hours of content uploaded every minute and more than 1 billion users, YouTube has become an invaluable addition to the classroom that cannot be ignored. This workshop will help you start curating and creating videos so you can start using right away. Let us walk you through the many ways you can use the site safely and effectively in your classroom. In this workshop, you will have hands-on and practical activities that include:

      ▶ Effectively search and find useful videos

      ▶ Create, embed and share playlists

      ▶ Explore privacy settings when uploading content

      ▶ Customize a Channel to host your content, playlists and more

      ▶ Produce and publish your own content through screencasting

▶ **Private Label**—Patrick Green can customize a workshop to fit your school's specific needs.

2. Take the Online Course

▶ **YouTube in the Classroom**

3. Attend an EdTechTeam Summit featuring Google for Education in your area.

**For more information visit
EdTechTeam.com/books**

**To request a workshop or for more info
contact press@edtechteam.com**

 facebook.com/YouTubeClassroom

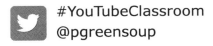 #YouTubeClassroom
@pgreensoup

 YouTube.com/pgreensoup

 YouTubeClassroom.com

About the Author

Patrick Green is an Education Technology Coordinator and Site Director for the Global Online Academy for the Singapore American School. He dreams of a world where people no longer use the word "technology," and instead talk about and seamlessly integrate "relevant tools" into their learning practice. Patrick thrives in the diverse connections his careers offers. He works enthusiastically with students, parents, teachers, and community stakeholders to help them meaningfully create, collaborate, communicate, and critically think.

Having taught in the Pacific Northwest, the Czech Republic, and now Singapore, Patrick is completing his twentieth year as an educational leader. He continues to find his inspiration first and foremost as a learner. He is an Apple Distinguished Educator, Principal's Training Center Trainer, Google Certified Innovator, Google Education Trainer, Common Sense Digital Citizenship Certified Educator, Google Street View Trusted, and a YouTube Star Teacher.

70479095R00058

Made in the USA
San Bernardino, CA
02 March 2018